STAIR-RODS AND STARS

By Adam Colton

A Cycling Perambulation

A CIP catalogue record for this book is available from the British Library

ISBN 978-1-5136-0525-8

Copyright © Adam Colton 2015

Classification: NON-FICTION

First Published in Great Britain in 2015 by Adam Colton, Hamstreet, Kent, UK

Front cover image: 'Glamping' near Appledore, Kent
Back cover image: Goodworth Clatford, Hampshire

For more information on digital and physical copies of Adam Colton's books email hamcopublishing@aol.com

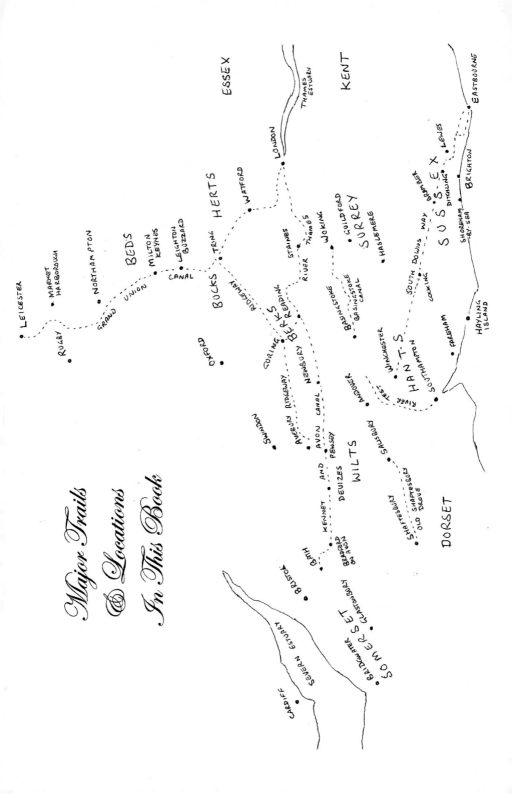

Major Trails & Locations In This Book

CONTENTS

PROLOGUE

How did it all begin?

I like to imagine that the seeds for this book were sewn back in 2006, when I did a kind of 'deal with the devil.' The devil in question was my friend Tom, who accompanied me on a hike from an obscure village in Kent to an obscure village in Somerset, armed with little more than a two-man tent and an axe.

Folklore has it that the legendary bluesman Robert Johnson exchanged his soul at a crossroads in return for his guitar playing prowess – a kind of Matrix-style download straight into the brain, courtesy of Lucifer. If he is currently burning in purgatory or worse, I imagine he wishes he'd skipped the international acclaim part and become an accountant, or whatever the 1930s equivalent of the most boring job in the world might be. I can say this; I did this job once!

During that two week hike, I imagined a metamorphosis taking place – I would return super-confident at having survived two weeks of extreme hiking and sleeping in the woods, powered up and ready to commence 'The Life of Adam Part II.'

But as with all the best plans, the trade-off was something different. Tom and myself merely swapped brains. Tom's aim at the time was to reject society's norms and pursue the 'Easy Rider' style dream of travelling from place to place, whereas I quite fancied meeting a nice girl and living the prescribed 'balanced' lifestyle.

Almost a decade on from that fateful walk, Tom is now married with two children, whilst my fiancée is from a country that the UK is only slightly more friendly with than North Korea or Syria. Aside from this, I spend much of my free time cycling from town to town and camping in the nearest wood, or failing that, copse or hedge.

And so, I give to you my experiences, seeking out the cycleways of Southern England, waking up to birdsong and gazing up through the trees from a warm sleeping bag, hoping that those aren't rain-clouds overhead.

Keen cyclists will find plenty of route suggestions here, as well as routes to avoid, whilst normal people can merely chuckle at the anecdotes from the warmth and comfort of a cosy room.

BASINGSTOKE CANAL

1) Bawdy Basingstoke

The easiest way to write this book is in reverse chronology, in the hope that more recent memories will create a kind of seismic brain-wave, loosening the memories of earlier trips, a bit like an archaeological dig through one's own cranium. If you've ever seen the Christopher Nolan directed film 'Memento' you will see the kind of effect I am hoping to achieve – a kind of gradual revelation, making sense of the earlier material, which is actually the later material, as things go on. What you'll probably get instead is a collection of unrelated, beer-clouded memories.

Our story begins on a reasonably sunny September morning. It was a Saturday and my local rail line in Kent was closed for engineering works (nothing new there), so I caught the 'replacement bus' to the town of Ashford and boarded my train from there. Not heard of Ashford? Don't worry, you will do. By 2030 it is predicted to be Kent's largest town. A local songwriter humorously wrote an ode to the town along the lines of 'Come to Ashford before Ashford comes to you.'

I unchained my bike, pleased to see that no joker had decided to let down my tyres or buckle my wheels (they say there's not a lot to do in Ashford), but I was less pleased to see a huge dollop of bird excrement across one of the handlebars. I pulled up some large leaves from the ground and tried to wipe the off-white substance away without touching it. However, it had the texture of oil and seemed to cling tenaciously to the rubber hand-grip. As a result, I can imagine a situation where somebody could ask, "Oi, is that bike for sale, mate?" to which I'd reply, "No, there's already a deposit on it!"

As you can see, I've decided to aim high at beginning of this book with that perennial favourite topic of bird's mess. You've still time to bail out and pick up the latest Dan Brown or something. But you're not going to do that, are you? To be honest, I am using the topic as a lure to get you to keep reading. It's like the worm on the end of the hook, except that the worm on *my* hook has already been digested!

My journey to Woking continued via the slow train to London Waterloo, which Southeastern, the rail operator, tactfully terms 'the mainline,' as opposed to the more expensive 'high speed' train that gets you from Ashford to London in half the time and empties your wallet at a similar velocity. As I sat waiting for the Woking train to depart Waterloo, I experienced an announcement which was bordering on comatose, with each word seeming as though it was being extracted via a syringe, syllable by syllable. The woman with the buffet trolley smiled and I suggested that the guard sounded like he needed a coffee.

And so I alighted, just outside the M25, in Woking – Surrey's second most populated town after Guildford. The narrow street leading away from the station had all the usual attractions – McDonald's, KFC, a kebab shop, etc. but I took the 'healthy' option of popping into a newsagent's for a samosa and a bottle of Lucozade.

Then it was time to begin the ride, cycling casually past the street leading to the main shopping centre and on across the dual carriageway to meet the Basingstoke Canal. This is now a 32-mile waterway, for it no longer makes it all the way to Basingstoke. It was completed in 1794 and was intended to serve the purpose of agricultural development in Hampshire. It begins a few miles back towards London at West Byfleet, where it departs from the Wey Navigation, which comes down southward from the River Thames. Note that a 'navigation' follows the route of an existing river, while a canal follows a completely man-made course.

The first part of my ride along the towpath was a suburban section, but eventually countryside encroached and a series of locks carried the canal towards the higher level of Farnborough. The scenery became more wooded as things went on, with lots of ferns and evergreen trees. The railway line was ever-present, but not ever-visible, to my left. Now and again a train rattled through, reminding me of its presence.

There seemed to be a children's sponsored run taking place on this day, so my sense of tranquillity was not quite what it could have been. Kids aren't the best at getting out of the way of 'cyclists on a mission,' so I got to exercise my vocal chords with plenty of calls of 'excuse me' and 'coming through on the left.'

This section of canal took a pretty straight course, and having climbed past the final lock in the series, it ran through a cutting and would remain at this level for the rest of its course (save for one lock at Ash). Appropriately named Deepcut, the military village nearby hit the headlines in the early noughties (as fashionable people used to call the first ten years of the third millennium) for the fact that there were four deaths due to gunshot wounds between 1995 and 2002 at the Princess Royal Barracks.

The canal then opened out twice into expansive lakes as it rounded a corner and began to head southward at the eastern edge of the town of Farnborough. I was now in Hampshire and there was a miniature railway line to my right. As I moved on, gardens of middle class houses lined the opposite bank and the most notable thing was a chap doing some kind of DIY job with a gazebo, suddenly letting out a hearty exclamation as I cycled past. For crossword fanatics out there: 'pair of male glands, 8 letters, begins with B.'

The word was then repeated in a slightly quieter tone afterwards for added pathos. Much as I have tried to circumnavigate printing the word myself, I understand that this was even uttered in an episode of the USA children's cartoon The Flintstones. It was one of those 'did I just hear that right?' moments, like when Rage Against the Machine's expletive laden rock track, 'Killing in the name of,' was played unexpurgated on BBC Radio 1's weekly 'top 40' chart rundown in the early nineties. The song returned with a vengeance to become Christmas number one in 2009, ousting the annual X Factor / karaoke single from the coveted position, but this time around the staff at the Beeb were more careful I am sure, although ironically the potency of the F-word has no doubt been diluted over this period by seventeen years of late evening chat show usage before an invited audience who shriek and applaud at every emanation.

Whilst I am not a fan of gratuitous swearing, the song does muster a justified level of defiance in its lyrics which seem to be aimed at racist organisations such as the Ku Klux Klan, although they could easily apply to any authoritarian group or regime. I don't see any of the X Factor finalists dealing with such weighty issues, so the position at number one seems deserved.

This is going to sound old-mannish, but we do seem to be living in a cultural vacuum. I wonder if a subversive songsmith such as the young Bob Dylan would get anywhere in today's climate, even if the message was delivered in a modern style. Although, that said, listen to the lyrics of the Black Eyed Peas' 2003 hit 'Where is the love?' a little bit closer and you'll see that the odd thinking person's lyric does slip through the net now and again.

The canal route became less attractive as I continued, with a feel of abandonment creeping in. A plane was coming in low to land at Farnborough Airport as I pedalled onward. The aqueduct over the dual carriageway perked up my interest again. By now, the canal had resumed a westbound course, running to the north of Aldershot. The next town I encountered was Fleet, a settlement which generously gives its name to a service area on the mighty M3 motorway. I decided to leave the banks of the waterway and explore a bit.

The town centre comprises a long, straight street, with all the usual stores. There was a market square by the side of the road, but I soon found myself gravitating towards an outlet of a well known pub-chain. I ordered a pint of a local ale at a refreshing price (about a third less than your average pub) and sat down at a table near the back of the room.

It was time to torment a few people, as I took a photo of my pint and sent it to my girlfriend and two other friends. It was 'beer o'clock.' As certain friends of mine might say, I was 'living the dream,' so I made sure this phrase was liberally used in my captions to rub it in further. You could call this going on a 'smarm offensive.'

Feeling invigorated, I then took a wander up the main street to see what else was on offer. In a decadent moment, I popped into a branch of Marks and Spencer and settled upon a luxury king prawn and avocado sandwich. I was on holiday, so what the hell? Resuming my route, I paused at two different points to consume this flamboyant snack.

As I left the town, I passed a beer garden which sloped down from the canal to a pub, before continuing into the land of the trees, not even noticing where the River Hart crosses the canal. To be honest, I was expecting another aqueduct, but the only thing to really grab my attention here was a World War II pillbox. I took a look inside this small, brick structure, using the torch on my mobile phone to see, as I wandered around behind the entrance wall.

The canal's course was rather idiosyncratic at this point, with a huge 'ox-bow' taking place, so I temporarily lost my bearings. A bright red sign then instructed me to leave the towpath, which was closed ahead due to a landslip.

I took the trackway out to the Church Lane, passing a residence, before riding the tarmac to the village of Dogmersfield. The weather clearly wasn't playing ball now, with a thin drizzle steadily emanating from the now-grey sky, creating a slight haze over the open fields.

Beyond the village, another wide lane led me back to the canal and I entered a small parking area from which I could pick up the towpath again. I had a sense that the rain was going to intensify, so I kept my eyes open for suitable places that I could shelter under my tarpaulin for an hour or two should it become too much.

My backpack contained very little on these trips usually – apart from small items like a toothbrush and some writing paper, the bulk of the contents were a tarpaulin, a sleeping bag and a jacket. The idea behind all my trips is to travel as light as possible, because 'weight being carried on the back' is always in inverse proportion to 'enjoyment gained from the ride.'

Mentally, I was set on the goal of reaching Basingstoke, finding an outlet of a familiar pub chain and enjoying a nice chicken tikka (I know the menu off by heart in these places, you see). But now I wondered if this aim would be attainable. Still, I was outdoors, I was free and this was a million times better than work, so there was no need to start getting all negative!

In fact, it was nice to see the odd narrowboat gracefully navigating the canal at this point (note, these should not be confused with barges, which are wider vessels usually used for carrying cargo). At the beginning of my ride the surface had seemed quite heavily covered in algae, but by now things were becoming more touristic. Many of the boats were tied up at the side and covered in tarpaulin, presumably having been 'put to bed' for the winter, but there is always something quite reassuring about not being the only tourist out enjoying the canal when the rain begins to patter. I noticed a bird wading at the side at one point too, but I couldn't say if it was a stork or a heron. Probably neither.

It seemed that the 'bark' of the weather was worse than its bite, as this turned out to be just a brief shower. Soon a main road opted for a parallel course to my right, and the rush of traffic could now be heard. I decided to leave via the next bridge and get some sustenance from the village of North Warnborough. In truth, I didn't really see any of the village, as there was a garage right next to the bridge. I got a cup of vanilla coffee from the Costa machine and a Turkish Delight bar to wash it down. Or was it the other way round?

I then returned to the towpath and noticed that one of those annoying red signs was stating that beyond the bridge the path was too narrow for cyclists, disabled chariots and a number of other wheeled contraptions. I gave a metaphorical two fingers to this; I had cycled all the way from Woking and I had no intention of giving up on riding the last few miles just because some councillor had probably been grouchy one day about having to move six inches to let a cyclist pass. In fact I didn't notice any reduction in width compared to the previous sections I had cycled. Defiantly, I laid my bike down and found a bank covered in soft plant life on which to sit and consume my coffee and chocolate treat.

Generally I have found ramblers to be very tolerant towards cyclists. In the absence of a bell, I was having to resort to a polite 'excuse me' as I approached the backs of walkers, who would invariably stand aside as I passed thanking them profusely. I was half expecting some hostility, having passed the red sign nonchalantly, but I found the walkers to be just as obliging here as before. Occasionally I would lie and say, "My bell's been stolen," for this was far simpler than explaining the circumstances which led to me riding this bell-less bargain of a bike.

I knew I was approaching the final miles of the 'canal proper,' as the waterway was becoming rather overgrown with reeds at this point, and it wasn't long before the towpath began to lead upward and I knew that this was the end. I chained up my bike (a wise precaution even in the most remote location, as we shall see later) and tramped down a steep trail etched into the bank. At the bottom I could see the entrance to Greywell Tunnel.

The tunnel, roughly three quarters of a mile in length, is now disused, having collapsed in the middle in 1932. However, a dystopian scene for humans can be ideal for nature, for the tunnel is now a listed site due to the bat population that makes its home in the cave-like surroundings.

Returning to my bike, the towpath ran over the mouth of the tunnel and led me out to a lane. There was a pub at a T-junction nearby, with a red phone box near the entrance. This was clearly there to enhance the rustic English scene. It's funny how a red phone box can seem quaint and picturesque, but if somebody wanted to erect a red sign near our homes we would say it was gaudy and unsightly.

I briefly, and slightly illegally, pedalled up a footpath which roughly followed the course of the tunnel, but when I reached a gate which led to a meadow, I decided not to push my luck and returned to the lane. This ran round in a big semi-circle to the south of the tunnelled area, and presented me with my first proper climb of the trip, raising my breath intake and providing some light cardio-vascular exercise. The scenery consisted of open, rolling fields, and the views were quite expansive, giving me a sense of being fairly high up.

I descended once again, and branched off of the lane to the right, to run down a gradually narrowing track, which led me back into woodlands, before sharply rounding the point where the west portal of the tunnel would have been, and descending to run beside the north bank of this now-derelict section of the canal.

This final mile or two had a distinct look of decay about it. The canal was now algae-ridden and overgrown with an all-pervading smell of dampness, yet once again, these were ideal conditions for wildlife to thrive in, and the area is regarded as a nature reserve. I passed beneath a few more bridges, rounded a bend where a short channel departed and soon found myself back beside the lane. Although the canal used to continue to Basingstoke, this really was the end. That chicken tikka was getting closer.

The roar of traffic on the M3 grew louder as the lane drew near and finally bridged it. Then I turned left, down beside a small industrial estate and crossed the A30 near a tempting looking pub. The next lane ran straight to the heart of Old Basing, a large village located a few miles to the east of Basingstoke. Turning left at the end of the lane, I passed some very old buildings as I wound my way through the trees towards the modern conurbation.

The lane was a dead end to cars, but provided a nice, quiet route for cyclists and walkers. Just before I passed beneath the subway under the dual carriageway, I had a look at the meadow next to the road. It was beginning to get dusky, so I thought I'd better have somewhere in mind for camping later on. There's nothing worse than cluelessly searching for a suitable spot in the dark, when you can't tell if you are well-hidden enough to be left alone by intruders or even if the ground is smooth enough to lay a groundsheet and sleeping bag upon.

I cleared away the fallen twigs from a bushy area in anticipation, but this would be a last resort, as camping in any kind of proximity to a river is not advised due to the abundance of gnats. I regularly camp in a private wood with some friends of mine and the late summer period is notorious for the little blighters. The experience of 'getting gnatted,' as we call it, is virtually synonymous with camping at this time of year.

I returned to the road and headed through the subway, into a strip of lakes and parkland that reminded of the then-futuristic '2015' version of Hill Valley in the Back to the Future films. I was half expecting Biff Tannen to come flying at me on a hoverboard at any moment. Above the trees you could see the modern office buildings of the town centre, looming over the place like corporate guardians.

I pressed on, past a shopping centre and headed up the pedestrianised road leading to Winchester Street, which forms

Basingstoke's central thoroughfare, now superseded by many a bypass. All the usual suspects were there, from McDonald's to Wetherspoons. I headed for the latter. Meanwhile, a group of tramps were sitting in the central square consuming alcohol and making quite a lot of noise. It was Saturday night in Basingstoke and these guys weren't going to be left out!

The pub was quite discretely located, as I cycled straight past it initially. The choices of ale seemed to be generally pretty strong (unless you are a fan of the ubiquitous Doom Bar brand). The pint I selected was a meaty 5.5% alcohol, but went down surprisingly easy. I took a seat beneath a screen which was pumping out the latest turmoil from an agonised world in silence with subtitles ('BBC news on mute' in other words).

I sat beneath it so that I could concentrate on my notes for this book undisturbed by bombing, abuse, sadism, murder, violence, corruption, and all the other wonderful things that this planet has to offer. Excusing my cynicism, I do sometimes wonder if humanity is akin to an experiment that has gone horribly wrong. Is it really worth the cost in sheer suffering to have 'intelligent' life on earth?

In a universe of billions of galaxies, each containing billions of stars, it is highly likely that intelligent life exists elsewhere. There should be civilisations millions of years more advanced than our own, but none have yet been able to reach us across the vast tracts of space and time (as far as we know). One explanation is that as soon as intelligent life evolves, it wipes itself out.

Humans (and all life) ultimately consist of the matter from exploded stars. With the knowledge we have, we are simply the universe observing itself, as a famous scientist once put it. Yet, we are too busy squabbling over oil, land, power, money, etc. to even notice what a miracle our existence is. We've far more important things to do, such as killing one another for improvable ideas and fanatical beliefs in the systems that control our lives.

Seriously, every edition of the news should come with a government health warning, telling us not to watch if we are prone to depressive thoughts. Or any kind of thoughts, come to think of it. If you can sit passively, without reacting to the sheer horror unfolding on the screen, then you are healthily adjusted to modern life. If not, the Pink Floyd lyric from The Wall will fit you aptly: "The prisoner who now stands before you / was caught red handed showing feelings / showing feelings of an almost human nature / this will not do!"

As I sat there, an old man with the world's most persistent cough chockupped his way through a pint of beer. I decided to order the traditional chicken tikka, served with a naan bread, poppadom and mango chutney. Traditional for me, that is. I was soon completely satiated, and the map on my phone showed an area of woodland to the north of the town. This would be my first choice for a campsite tonight. It was now dark, so I needed to be absolutely sure about my route.

As I left, the 'wino men' had piped down. I grabbed my bike and set off down the street and across a footbridge, over one of Basingstoke's many large, central roads. The town is home to the headquarters of the Automobile Association, so this car-dominated layout seems fitting I would guess.

My route passed beneath the railway lines and then climbed a suburban hill, where I called into a corner shop for an emergency chocolate bar, in case I woke up famished in the night. When you're in the wilds of Greater Basingstoke, you've got to take all provisions. It's a jungle out there.

I then continued via various housing estates and cruised through a subway under another dual carriageway. This had an almost surreal feel, as I speeded through the oblong of yellow light and back out into the darkness beyond. When I came to the most northerly of the town's east-west roads, I located the track that led up into the evergreen woodland. Upon reaching a junction point, I headed off into the trees at an acute angle and picked a suitably secluded spot to camp.

Out came the groundsheet and onto it went the sleeping bag, and before long I was gazing up through the branches, expecting to hear nothing but silence, as you would in a forest at night. Yet, somewhere in another corner of the wood, some youths were having a whale of a time. Drink induced laughter echoed through the woods from both male and female specimens. This eventually died down and soon sleep came, like a wave crashing through the brain and sweeping away the last vestiges of awareness in a shimmery kind of semi-consciousness.

2) Farnborough Freak-out

As the night went on a gentle breeze got up. I woke up many times, but as daylight crept through the woodland, human voices began to appear in the same way that birdsong does. This time a man was continually shouting, at regular intervals of roughly ten seconds. The shout consisted of a name, presumably that of a wayward dog, followed by 'come on!' every second time. This continued for around an hour.

Now, if you do the maths, that is 360 shouts of the dog's name and 180 shouts of 'come on!' Yet, remarkably, after all this time I still wasn't sure of the dog's name. It sounded like 'Heathcote.' The note inflexion was always that of a slight drop in tone between the first and second syllable. Quite frankly, it sounded unnatural, obsessional and pretty weird, and if I was the dog I would have bit my owner's leg in order to get a different sound to emerge from his vocal chords.

Once I decided to rise from the warmth and comfort of the sleeping bag, I brushed my teeth, wolfed down my chocolate bar and decided to do a lap of the woodland.

The track headed northward, with a few right-angle bends punctuating the long straights, and most people said 'good morning,' which I liked. When the track seemed to run out, I had a look at the map on a board, but I seemed a bit disorientated. Now when I go camping with those friends of mine, we usually spend a small fortune on beer and wine to achieve this effect, but here I'd achieved it for free.

I took a narrower path back and eventually came out into a small housing estate. The trusty 'map app' on my phone then led me back to the town centre. I took a roughly similar route to last night, but this time I went around the edge of a square green near a school. Once back in the economic epicentre of exotic Basingstoke, I used all the imagination I could muster, and headed back to The Maidenhead Inn. It seemed the simplest option for breakfast on a Sunday morning after all.

The cup of tea went down like a snake's foot. Yes, I know it's a funny saying, but my camping buddies use it a lot, usually in the context of necking down some beer or wine. Apparently members of their family have used this saying for many years, so they are determined that this time-honoured tradition won't end with them. I am doing my best to help them, but it's not really catching on.

The breakfast could have done with about an extra twenty degrees centigrade, but it was still pretty good. It was then time for today's mission – to return to Woking, retracing my route from yesterday, but cutting out some of the lengthy deviations in the meandering course of the canal. And so, it was back through the 'Back to the Future' park, under the subway, around the long bend past my original idea for a campsite and out via the large village of Old Basing.

Before long, I had bridged the motorway and passed through the small village of Up Nately on the lane – I decided to skip the wild 'nature reserve' canal section and get a good run-up on the lane for the substantial climb. I turned right after the pub with the phone box in Greywell, and rather than pick up the canal I followed the lanes to Odiham. This village surprised me, as once I'd crossed the B-road and entered the wide, central street, it seemed more like a small town. There was even a bank. I mean, how many villages have banks these days?

I spotted a wooden notice-board that was crying out to have one of my business cards pinned onto it. I always carry a few of these to try to promote my books at any given opportunity. They don't seem to have done a lot for sales, but I did meet my future wife through one. More of that later.

At a roundabout, I crossed the A287 and took a dead end lane back to the canal. There were a further two notice-boards along here, so I graced both of them with an addition. I was in a hamlet of well-to-do houses, with open meadows and woodlands beyond. From the bridge, I descended to the towpath, and soon I was again calling out 'coming through on the left' or 'excuse me' to nonchalant dog-walkers, occasionally apologising for the lack of bell on the bike I was riding.

This £10 marvel had been sold to me by the aforementioned camping 'dudes.' Having lost my mountain bike which had carried me for literally thousands of miles and for the duration of every trip recorded in this book, except this one, they took pity on me and offered me a bargain, but it was a bell-less bargain nonetheless.

A splendid weeping willow draped over the ribbon of water from a garden at the point where a big red sign instructed me to leave the towpath because of the landslip. Remember that?

So I was back on the road to Dogmersfield, which had the interesting name of Chatter Alley. I must have shaved off about four miles as I continued via Crookham Village and on towards the outskirts of Fleet. I picked up the towpath again from here and stayed on it right the way through the town, stopping to eat the other chocolate bar from the two-pack and pocketing the (w)rapper. For those aged over 40, who didn't get the pun, Tupac was a famous rapper, long after the golden era of pop and rock with real musical instruments requiring considerable manual dexterity to play.

At the eastern edge of Fleet, a roundabout straddled the canal across two bridges, but I didn't recall seeing any route up to it the day before, so I took a short cut through an area of woodland, climbing steadily as I pushed my bike over the soft ground beneath conifer trees, to emerge onto the road at the top.

On my map, a dead straight line ahead would lead me towards the next destination of Farnborough. Now, up until this point the weekend had been a success and everything had gone swimmingly, but it seems that I was about to seamlessly enter a parallel universe, where everything seems identical, but the 'karma' is most definitely worse.

I quite like this theory concerning when things unexpectedly go bad, because of course it means they can unexpectedly change for the better again – like drifting between two parallel universes of yin and yang. But not today – today there was just yin and more yin. (Or maybe yang and more yang. I'm not sure which one is the unpleasant one – maybe they take it in turns.)

With travel writing I have often noticed that the more unpleasant the author's experience is, the more entertaining the writing will be. Well, maybe if I make this next section as boring as possible and therefore attempt to break this rule, fate will throw less crud at me on future jaunts. Some hope!

So I cruised down a long slope, with evergreen woodland to my left and a huge wire-netting fence to my right. Just beyond a T-junction, the lane abruptly ended at a security gate, leading into what seemed to be an aeronautical operation.

I backtracked to try the road that had departed at the junction, but this was a dead end leading to a sports area. A football match was in progress and I followed a couple who were walking around the edge of the pitch and asked them the easiest route out, accompanying my request for info with the statement, "It's like Fort Knox around here."

There was no way out other than the way I'd arrived, so my attempt to shave off some mileage from the canal route was already proving futile. However, I was having none of this and I decided to venture along a path through the woodland instead, but this then went beneath the Fleet West Bypass road that I wanted to get up onto, so I eventually dragged my bike through a forest of fern and leapt over a barbed wire fence to get onto it. 'Has the equilibrium been restored?' I wondered.

The answer came in the form of an angry blast from a car horn. The driver was presumably communicating his incandescent rage that a cyclist was daring to use the carriageway when there was a parallel cycle path. Cycle path or psychopaths? If the driver had waited a few more seconds before blowing his top, he would have observed that I had already chosen the cycleway option and was merely waiting for a flat kerb to get up onto it.

And so to Farnborough.

The approach was all industrial estates and buildings associated with the airport. A dead straight path beside the busy road carried me forward via a succession of roundabouts. The centre of Farnborough seemed to be a centrifuge of gyrating traffic. By now, I was looking for a nice pub for a quiet pint, but 'quiet' definitely wasn't on the menu here.

I followed some young people with some rap music emanating from a mobile phone (why is it always rap?), across the series of pelican crossings necessitated by the road system.

I then headed eastward via a more tranquil road, lined with wealthy suburban houses, and emerged onto another north-south road, but here, there was more of a village feel. I spied a pub, chained my bike to a lamppost and entered.

There was a brief lull in the negative vibes as I ordered my pint, observing the cosy atmosphere of those enjoying a nice lunch. I headed through to the outside seating area at the back. This was surrounded by what I would describe as a plastic marquee. The area was clearly designed for smokers, a clever way to get around the smoking ban in pubs, enabling those who wish to imbibe of the nicotine to do so in relative comfort. My reason for being there was merely that I wanted to make a call to my girlfriend in Moscow in relative privacy.

If you're looking for a romantic aspect to this tale, this could be your lucky day. We had been doing the 'distance relationship' thing for several years. In that time our countries had entered a new Cold War and we were beginning to consider engagement. So we discussed what kind of rings might be appropriate for a cash-strapped situation such as ours (these flights aren't cheap you know), and I temporarily paused the call to purchase a second pint. It was one of those golden ales and it went down like that proverbial snake's foot.

Towards the end of my call, I wandered away from the smokers and around the side of the pub to say goodbye in more isolated surroundings. 'Why are we so shy in England?' I wondered, as my voice lowered to a virtual whisper. This learned shyness reminded me of that Pink Floyd lyric again about the perils of 'being caught red handed showing feelings.'

And this was when it all went catastrophically wrong. Following the end of the call, my phone decided to lock up. I tried to reset it by turning it off and on again, but I couldn't even shut it down because the 'slider' on the screen wasn't sliding. What's more, I could see that I had received a text message from my mother which I could neither read nor answer, risking throwing her into a catatonic state of worry.

'I hate technology!' I thought to myself as I left the pub, and I remember dropping it on the ground at one point to see if a good shake-up would do it any good. It didn't.

So I set off over the level crossing at Farnborough North station and used a path to bridge the main road and cross another railway line via another level crossing. I then asked a pedestrian where I could locate that most old fashioned of facilities – a phone box.

He directed me to a large, triangular green, with a good, old fashioned, red kiosk at the side, complete with the traditional smashed glass that I always remember from the halcyon days of the eighties – the golden age of vandalism! Just what is so fascinating about smashing every single one of those little, oblong panes of glass I have never understood. Surely, even the most mindless yob would smash about five and then think, 'This is getting a bit samey now!' Well, whoever had pummelled this particular box had decided enough was enough once all the door panes were smashed out, for all the panes in the sides of the kiosk were still blissfully intact. Nick Lowe used to sing "I love the sound of breaking glass," but you clearly *can* have too much of a good thing.

Anyway, I went inside and put 50p into the slot to find it spat straight back out again. Then I read the small print that the only way to use a phone box in the 21st century is to tap in your credit or debit card number and allow them to take a minimum fee for the privilege, even if you just want to say "I can't contact you because my mobile is broken." Now I was raging!

I slammed the receiver back onto the handle so that it fell off and was left dangling by its chord for a full thirty seconds while I stood outside the box and assessed my predicament. This assessment told me that the situation was 'pants' (to use a modern parlance) but also that I needed the phone box more than it needed me. Resisting the urge to shatter one of the remaining oblongs of glass with the receiver, I reluctantly began tapping in the sixteen digits from my debit card in order to have a brief exchange with my mum.

As for my girlfriend, who would no doubt end up equally worried over in Moscow, I would have to contact her when I got home, presumably by taking my laptop to the pub to use the local Wi-Fi. A great excuse for a beer at least.

By now, I had just one desire, to get to Woking and call into a phone shop to find out just how much cash I would have to part with in order to communicate with my friends and family again. It's like having your whole life held to ransom by technology. How did we ever get so reliant on these gadgets?

I followed the road signs to Woking, expecting to rejoin the canal towpath at a bridge, but I was clearly further north than I thought, as there was no bridge and no canal; just a series of B-roads which I powered my way along with the singular goal of finding that phone shop. I abandoned the idea of following the canal altogether and continued to veer away from it, blithely following the road signs. The scenery was fairly pleasant, with a long descent at one point, and plenty of woodlands disguising the generally densely populated nature of this area.

I passed through the village of Chobham, and before long I had covered the eight or nine miles to Woking with ease. I bridged the canal at the point where I'd first dropped down onto the towpath the day before, and headed for the centre. A young lady gave me rough directions to my mobile phone store of choice: "It's either in that shopping centre there or the other one."

As I explained the problem to the person at the counter, he warned me that a new screen would cost somewhere between 'stratospheric' and 'astronomical.'

'What?!'

But then, somehow, he managed to turn off the phone and reset it.

"How did you do that?" I asked, as though inquiring for the secret of the Indian rope trick from an esteemed magician.

"You just press those two buttons in simultaneously," came the response.

So all in all, 90% of the anguish could have been relieved with just a little more understanding of my gadget. Sadly for me, the weekend had been tarnished. The rage I'd felt in the phone box seemed to obliterate all the pleasure that went before; the balance sheet of enjoyment was reading zero. Initially I'd wanted to conclude the ride by heading further along the canal to West Byfleet to where it's course ends upon meeting the Wey

Navigation, which links the River Thames and Guildford, but my energy had been sapped and I merely trundled along to the station and began my journey home. You could say that I'd thrown in the towel.

A quick McDonald's burger killed the wait at Tonbridge in Kent and the rail replacement bus was late at Ashford, so I concluded that it would be quicker to face the music and cycle the last seven miles home, pounding my way down the notorious, accident ridden A2070 as dusk fell. This was my second consecutive biking trip that had ended on a low, but because we are going backwards in time, we have conveniently avoided ending this book with a whimper.

SOUTH DOWNS WAY (MID SECTION)

3) Sleepless in Shoreham

"Who wants to rewind?" was the familiar call of many a rave DJ in the 1990s, eliciting the hyped up crowd to cheer for a replay of a tune that wasn't really that great the first time around. Well, there is going to be a lot of rewinding in this book, as we gradually delve back further and further in time.

The trip I am about to recall took place three months earlier in June, and just like the last one, there is a sting in its tail. Those who have been paying attention should easily be able to guess what it is. I consciously avoid using the phrase 'Can you guess what it is yet?' these days, for fear of evoking memories of a disgraced childhood hero. It seems ironic really that children of the seventies were parentally steered away from classic rock music like Black Sabbath, etc. whilst Rolf and chums were considered good, wholesome entertainment. Sadly, it seems that so many of our childhood heroes needed to be given psychiatric help, not a TV series!

Perhaps the main punishment for entertainment's fallen idols is that they have since been effectively written out of history. All their creative endeavours have been voided by the fact that they were not the people we thought they were.

If a performer or artist has done something we find abhorrent, is there any pleasure still to be gained from their work? My natural reaction is an emphatic 'no,' and a pile of CDs usually finds its way out of my collection and onto the charity shelf at work whenever this happens, although I have since learned that the charity shelf doesn't want them either.

That said, I sometimes do wonder if we are consequently leaving a false illusion of our times, giving future generations an impression that our society is so fair that nobody predatory or manipulative ever succeeds, when in fact these could be the very characteristics that secured their fame and fortune in the first place. Sometimes its easier not to think.

Anyway, where was I? Oh yes, Sussex.

My mission this time was to complete a central section of the South Downs Way, roughly between the villages of Bramber and Cocking. 'The Way' is a 100-mile trail which follows an ancient ridgeway. The modern day trail connects Eastbourne, on the Sussex Coast, with Winchester in deepest Hampshire, predominantly running along the top of the scarp slope of England's 4th longest hill-range, which is now a national park. This means that one is treated to stunning views across The Weald of Southern England. Furthermore, unlike the North Downs Way, the route can be cycled in its entirety.

This section was a missing link for me. You will read about the western end of the route from Cocking to Winchester later in this book, and I had ridden the eastern end during a couple of day trips, namely from Ditchling to Bramber, and Ditchling to Eastbourne.

The Eastbourne end of the South Downs Way actually forms a loop. The southern part of this includes the breathtaking scenery of the Seven Sisters (a series of seven chalk cliffs overlooking the English Channel) as well as the notorious yet beautiful, Beachy Head. On one occasion I popped into the clifftop pub here and asked the barmaid if it was really true that they have to be on the look out for depressed people who look like they might do themselves in.

She confirmed that it was, and I asked how often the suicides took place, expecting her to say something like, 'Once or twice a year.' The reply was that virtually every day somebody attempts to leap and that there is a counselling service nearby, operating 24 hours a day for would-be jumpers. Well, on this day, I eschewed the option of taking in 600 feet of breathtaking scenery before being scattered across it and got straight into the nitty-gritty of cycling.

I'd actually travelled down to Shoreham-by-Sea straight after work. It is not the easiest thing to get out of work mode and into leisure mode without the aid of a pint or two, and there was no option for that on the non-buffet-car service to Brighton from Ashford.

Young girls, all dolled up for a night out in Brighton, boarded the train at Lewes and the noise level increased somewhat for this last ten miles. The next train was longer and quieter, although there was an altercation when a passenger brushed the handlebars of a bike and tutted. Unlike me, this cyclist was having no nonsense and challenged the guy about his surly attitude towards bikes.

As I alighted at Shoreham-by-Sea, I popped into a newsagent for a drink. Shoreham has a busy High Street running along what feels like a seafront but is actually the River Adur. The central area behind this is surprisingly quaint, with its quiet streets giving it the feel of a small, provincial town.

Emerging from the newsagent's, I decided to phone my mother for some advice. A well known disc jockey had invited us onto his Sunday afternoon radio programme to perform a few songs from our self-produced CD. However as I had now opted to disappear into deepest, darkest Sussex for the weekend, I was wondering if maybe we should have checked first. Potential careers can go down the pan over things like this.

I hastily typed out an email on my phone and sent it, before making my way to the cycle path that heads inland beside the River Adur. This is a monster of a route, which can be followed all the way to Guildford in Surrey. It predominantly follows the trackbed of two disused railway lines via Christ's Hospital (just to the west of Horsham) and the main bulk of the path forms The Downs Link which joins the South Downs Way to the North Downs Way. This was a route I was very familiar with from my 'day rides.' However, today, I wasn't going far at all, as it was about 9.30pm and getting dusky. All I needed for the moment was a suitable spot to dump my tarpaulin and sleeping bag and crash.

It seemed that the southern end of the path was hiding itself from me, so I headed northward on the main road. When I finally found a way onto the trail, I must have been a good half a mile north of its beginning point.

I passed beneath the swirling concrete fly-overs of the A27 junction and admired the stately presence of Lancing College across the muddy river, looking like a cathedral minus its tower. If you've got in excess of thirty grand that you need to dispose of annually, your son or daughter can board there. If you've only got a paltry £22,000 to fling about, then he or she will have to be a day pupil. If you have neither, you can be like me and grow up to do the kind of job where you don't need a thesaurus to explain what you do. Turning my nose up at such cossetted existences, I promptly dived into the hedge hoping to have found a suitable spot to camp.

I was surprised at how busy the path was in spite of the crepuscule (it's always good to get that word in at least once per book), so I had to wait for a few cyclists to pass each time before discreetly assessing a new 'hole.' I eventually settled on a spot beneath some spindly branches on the east side of the trackbed. It was here I could see that I was on an embankment due to the drop-off to the side of me. Unfortunately, even after all the other trips you will read of in this book, I still hadn't learned the golden rules of camping – always find a proper wood (or at least a copse), and never camp near a main road.

The noise from the A283 became increasingly annoying as time passed, with me constantly wondering when the rate of cars passing would finally drop. Midnight came and went, and the rush of vehicles continued. In the end I had to resort to earphones and ambient music. I put 'Selected Ambient Works' by Aphex Twin on to try to lull me to sleep, but unfortunately this deliberately soporific music was sufficiently interesting to keep me conscious.

For those not in the know, 'The Twin' was perhaps the first proponent of the exclusively nineties musical genre of 'blokes somewhere provincial mixing up tapes in their bedrooms.' In his case, the 'somewhere provincial' was Cornwall.

To be honest, I think the nineties were something of a brief creative renaissance in music, as things temporarily moved away from the mass produced corporate sounds of the eighties (music for twelve-year-olds if you want it in layman's terms). Ian MacDonald states in his book 'Revolution in the Head,' which analyses the songs of The Beatles, that the sixties were 'the last gasp of the western soul,' but maybe if we all pop up for another lungful every thirty years or so, things might not be so bad in the 2020s. I'm not holding my breath though.

I had just started to get that 'swimmy head' feeling that is usually a sign that sleep is about ten minutes away, so I pulled out my earphones to discover that the road had gone quiet. It was now gone 2am. But just as I finally embraced the prospect of getting some sleep, some kind of bird piped up, maybe a nightingale. The lumpy ground finally got to me and I abandoned the idea of sleep and instead gorged myself on some deli items I'd bought from a supermarket in Rye during my journey.

****

I obviously did get to sleep eventually, as I awoke at about 8am, staring up at a blue sky through the tangled weave of branches. Personally I think this is the best kind of ceiling to wake up beneath, as it means a day of freedom and sunshine awaits.

I packed up all my gear, stumbled out of the bushes across the nettles and weeds and rejoined the path, which was already thronging with cyclists. Back in the saddle, I continued my way northward.

The path made a sudden detour to the right at a point where the railway line would have bridged the river to run on the opposite side to the village of Bramber. The Downs Link path rejoins the trackbed a mile or so north of the village. However, this was not the trail I was following today, so at the point where the pathway bridges the river, I took a right turn to head back out to the road that had kept me awake half the night – the cantankerous A283.

At the roundabout where it streaks off to bypass the villages, I continued ahead into the village of Upper Beeding. This was familiar territory for me from riding the South Downs Way from Ditchling some years before.

Upper Beeding rolls seamlessly into Bramber, which is very quaint, with a bridge over the River Adur, a small central square and colourful flower baskets hanging from the awnings. I went up the slope to the church and abandoned my bike by the gate in order to wander around the ruins of the early twelfth century Bramber Castle.

The most striking part of the castle is an imposing, stone monolith that once formed the towering wall of the keep-gatehouse. This is set on a hill above the village and there are pleasant views across the flat farmland of the Adur Valley. I was surprised to learn that King John (of Magna Carta fame) was quite nasty in imprisoning the family of the baron who owned the castle and starving them. Much as I often criticise the 'haves' for having too much, I think starving them is a little drastic!

There was a fresh feel to the morning air as I wandered around the grassy remnants, and on the way back to my bike, I called in the church for a nose too. I then freewheeled down to our old friend, the A283, and crossed the roundabout to check out Steyning. This was another almost seamless merge of settlements, but of the three, Steyning is by far the biggest - a pleasant little country town.

Chaining my bike to a post in a car park, I then committed the grave offence of pulling the door of a public toilet open to reveal somebody in mid-flow. I apologised and he took it well, conceding that the lock didn't work properly.

I found an atmospheric café up a little alleyway, which seemed the perfect place for a 'full English' and a life-giving pot of tea. Music from the forties, fifties and sixties added to the ambience, and I heard one of my grandmother's favourite songs, Shady Nook (the signature song of Donald Peers), for the first time since I was a child - perhaps an apt choice given my penchant for such places as campsites. A well-spoken man in his sixties was reading a book at a table next to me. I imagined that he was perhaps an author himself.

The breakfast went down like a snake's foot (what else?) and after this I was ready to continue and face up to the monster climb onto the South Downs to begin riding my 'missing link' of the South Downs Way.

The till where you paid for your food and drink was on the way out. The girl was chatty and I explained that I was about to cycle to Cocking, to which she replied that she'd never even heard of the place. This told me just one thing – it was a long way!

So, I left the town via a narrow lane which climbed onto the hills to the south. The climb got steeper and steeper and the heat was beginning to get searing. I was amazed at the Lycra-clad cyclists who were streaking past me up the hill as I pushed my bike with head bowed, as though this streamlined positioning would make any difference at two miles per hour. I made a brief stop to admire the view halfway.

Once at the summit, things levelled out and the South Downs Way departed at a reflex angle so that I was almost doubling back on myself. This track presented me with a long, slow ascent back to the ledge of the scarp slope. It then curved round to run westward along this ridge. As I rode, everybody said 'Good Morning' and no less than three cyclists commented on the size of my rucksack. Little did they know that 90% of the bulk was taken up by my 'all weathers' sleeping bag.

The views were great and the trail ran across expansive, open grassland with the occasional copse overlooking The Weald below – very typical of 'South Downs Way' scenery in fact. My route curved past Chanctonbury Ring, an Iron Age hill-fort, identifiable by its cluster of beech trees to the right of the path. Weirdness abounds here, with tales of summoning the devil and extra-terrestrial activity in abundance.

One such legend is that if you run around the ring seven times anti-clockwise (why is it always seven?), the devil will turn up with a bowl of soup in return for your soul. Thinking back to the preface, if Robert Johnson got a career as one of the most famous blues musicians of all time, a bowl of soup seems a pretty paltry offering, unless it's mulligatawny perhaps. Another legend is that the devil himself created the ring as a by-product of another construction project nearby. He was a busy little thing in those days. In my opinion these legends are a load of old hogwash really, but they still make interesting stories.

I soon found myself drawn into a 'hare and tortoise' style race with a pair of male cyclists who kept overtaking me, only for me to pass them again each time they stopped. When I reached the point where the trail branched right to descend and cross the A24, they notified me that my back light was on. 'How did that get turned on?' I wondered. Perhaps the devil had been up to mischief after all.

The descent was stony, and I had to cross the dual carriageway before a lane began the ascent back onto the ridge. This became another gravelly track, and a water tap had been thoughtfully positioned near the bottom. I had a short rest and rehydrated myself.

The climb beyond was entirely rideable, being a long, steady incline with no 'shock' gradients. Near the top I passed a lot of poppies, and the views, as ever, were superlative. To my right, way below, I could see the large village / small town of Pulborough and the meandering River Arun. As I rode on I could see the B-road way below me, running parallel to the hills accompanied by a line of scattered houses.

But as always with this ancient trackway, what goes up must come down, and soon I was plunging into the Arun Valley. The descent got steeper and steeper, until it was just a chalky straight line down the hillside. I couldn't believe that a middle aged cyclist was stoically pedalling towards me, meandering his way up this near vertical ascent. As I plunged into trees, I noticed that my recently acquired pair of ophthalmic sunglasses seemed to make the descent appear steeper still. I almost panicked and walked.

When I reached the road at the bottom, the path turned right to run in a separate channel between hedges, until emerging onto the tarmac. I worried that this section could be riddled with thorns from when the hedges were cut – a potential puncture risk, which is the single most annoying thing you can get on these rides.

I swiftly decided that a pint was in order, and a helpful sign directed me to the village of Amberley. As I turned off the fast paced B-road, I passed a playing field and then found myself in a world of thatched cottages, which lined the two narrow streets, providing a scene that wouldn't look out of place on a box of fudge. The village was very quaint indeed, but alas, the Black Horse pub was closed. I turned left again and eventually found the lane descending beside the huge walls of a castle. I took a short wander along the footpath at the end of the road, but it was something of a wilderness, so I doubled back, returned via the village to the B-road and continued west on the South Downs Way.

This section took me over the railway line (which runs north from Arundel), and continued beside the meandering River Arun before bridging it, crossing a lane and then shifting back into 'vertical mode' for another climb back onto the hills. The trail was chalky and stony now, as it zigzagged its way towards the stratosphere. Needless to say, I was pushing my bike in that hunchback style again. The sun was searing now and the perspiration was flowing as surely as the mighty River Arun.

Near the top there was a woodland to the right of the path. I dived in and sat down behind a fallen tree trunk to enjoy the cool shade and the remnants of the food and drink I was carrying. This seemed an ideal place for a camp, ticking all the boxes such as easy access, a nice smooth surface to lay down upon and seclusion from prying eyes. As we shall see, such sites usually present themselves in the middle of the day and rarely as dusk approaches, when one often has to head for the nearest hedge.

Emerging from this haven of coolness, I continued skyward on the trail, crossing the A29 (basically the Bognor Regis to London road). Yet, it wasn't long before I found 'The Way' descending into a diagonal valley. When I reached the bottom, another epic climb commenced, first through trees and then through merciless direct sunlight.

The trail hairpinned to the right halfway up this stony ascent towards Bignor Hill. It was after this that I reached a junction of paths, one of which was the Roman road, Stane Street. Further north, the A29 follows this characteristically straight route which links Chichester and London, but at this point it was just a trail through the coppiced woodland. I sat down on a wooden seat for a bit before the final push to 'publand.'

Not long after this 'The Way' began to descend again, with more great views of the formidable hills beyond the valley. As I neared the bottom I asked a lady for directions to the nearest alehouse. My heart sank at the words 'two miles' – by now I was gasping for life-giving beer.

Upon reaching the A285 road, I turned right. There were expansive green hillsides on either side, but it soon became apparent that this valley was still quite high, as the road nosedived off of the scarp slope with some sharp bends to lessen the gradient. At the bottom it curved around a bit through the scattered village of Duncton and descended some more, until eventually I reached the pub, located on a sweeping bend where the road had clearly been realigned a little further away from the buildings.

There were three real ales to choose from (tick) and a wedding reception was taking place. At first I had mixed feelings about this, as generally people in suits and smart dresses don't talk to strangers, and I was just about to sup up and move on when a man in his twenties called Luke came and chatted, curious about my adventure.

Slowly we drifted into politics and he expressed his disdain for the kind of views expounded by Rupert Murdoch and chums (tick) and his disapproval of 'fracking' (tick). That's 'hydraulic fracturing' in case you've been on Mars for a few years, and at the time this was the Government's hope for securing Britain's power supply by releasing natural gas from the ground beneath our homes. All in all I see the logic in wanting to be less dependent on oil from countries that don't like us much, but isn't it bizarre that one minute we are all worrying for our lives due to climate change and the next minute we are being told that pouring chemicals into the ground and releasing large quantities of gas is the future, and that wind-farms, solar panels, etc. are all a waste of time? These politicians must think we have the memory span of a budgerigar.

Reluctantly, Luke went in to get some food from the buffet, so I moved towards the bar and got chatting to a guy called John. It is strange how you can spot a teacher from a mile off. He had that look of measured casualness, and coupled this with a calm, left wing elucidation which together hinted at his vocation.

A girl called Catherine who was one of the bridesmaids (well, she was wearing the same dress as the others at least) then joined us. She was perhaps in her late twenties and was active with a road safety campaign in nearby Pulborough. As had happened with Luke, the three of us gradually drifted onto politics. We concluded our healthy bout of government bashing with the observation that in the rural South-East (where as a friend once put it 'most people are only slightly to the left of Genghis Khan') it was something of a minor miracle for three kindred spirits who had never met before to find themselves metaphorically tearing our illustrious leaders a new mouthpiece.

When both of them had left, a guy called Dave bought me half a pint. It would have been a whole pint but sensibility was starting to kick in and I knew I had to leave soon or I would end up staying in this pub all evening. I sat on a bench outside before finally breaking free of the strong gravitational force keeping me at this pub. I grabbed my bike and pedalled off up the main road in the direction of Petworth.

This was just under four miles, and after more undulations the road made a long, straight, gentle climb from the flat, open fields to the town centre. Like the aforementioned Pulborough, Petworth is a small, attractive town. There is a one way system at the centre where the road is channelled beside the high wall of the National Trust owned Petworth House and Park. The mansion was famously featured in the paintings of Turner.

The centre of the town has a few scattered shops and a car park which has the feel of a market square. I eventually located a Chinese restaurant and ordered that most Chinese of foods, an omelette and chips. I then took this to a bench by the car park and voraciously consumed about 80% of this gargantuan portion. The town was very quiet, with just a few people serenely walking past with dogs – perhaps the best excuse to get away from that cursed TV and out for an evening wander.

The brick wall of tiredness then hit me, and I was beginning to feel the strain in my legs as I continued northward in search of a suitable place to kip. I spied a long copse beside the main road as I left the town and immediately dived in. It was another substandard choice as far as I was concerned, but I really couldn't have continued any further.

I kicked down the nettles and lay my tarpaulin and sleeping bag down on the ground, suitably far away from the murky looking stream and its inevitable plethora of gnats, and before I knew it I was in the land of Nod.

However, medical advice proved itself to be true, that whilst alcohol can get you off to sleep quicker, the quality declines as the night goes on. I was awake for some significant time within the night, and the proximity of the main road meant that my sleep was broken with every car roaring through the darkness along this straight section; the drivers opening up their engines like wild animals released from the 30-limit of Petworth. 'Maybe Catherine's point about the drivers in Pulborough could be extended to West Sussex in general,' I mused.

4) Crisis at Chichester

'Aaaaarrrgggh no!' I thought as I finally awoke for good at 8am. The idea of this trip was supposed to be a healthy excursion, but it had turned into a pub crawl and I had violated my self-imposed advisory 3.5 pint limit by quite a margin. I'd arrived at this rather precise figure because the official definition of 'binge drinking' at this time was set at anything over eight units (or four pints) per session, and as they don't sell beer in third-pints or quarter-pints/gills, this is the maximum one can imbibe whilst still remaining puritanical in the eyes of the Government.

A craving for water ensued, or at least some kind of liquid that didn't contain alcohol, so I packed up my stuff, wandered out to the main road and headed back into the centre of Petworth.

I bought a chicken and bacon wrap and a bottle of bitter lemon drink from a Co-op shop and enjoyed this makeshift breakfast sitting on the steps of what seemed to be a town hall type building. I pondered over the remaining salami slices, and whether or not they were fit to eat after being carried around in a boiling rucksack for a day. Luckily they fell out of the packet onto the ground, neatly alleviating me of this culinary dilemma.

It was then time to return to the hills, from whence I came, so with backpack donned, I retraced the main road back past the pub which had turned my adventure into something bordering on hedonism, and up through Duncton once again. The road turns sharply left before the steep part of the climb begins, and I turned right onto a dead end lane to the hamlet of East Lavington.

With the scarp slope covered in woodland to my left, I passed a few isolated dwellings and eventually found myself beside a little church. I left my bike on the dirt bank beside the lane, which was now just a stony trail, and climbed to take a look inside.

It seemed that the church was next to the grounds of a stately home as I gazed down across neatly mowed lawns from the church door. A little research reveals that Lavington House is part of the Seaford College complex, situated not in Seaford as you might expect, but in the beautiful grounds of Lavington Park.

The idea that my bike might not be there when I returned had never even crossed my mind, and sure enough, I was soon brushing the mud from the handlebars before beginning to push it up the long, slow climb back onto the hills.

The byway ran between steep banks at one stage and the forest provided some much-needed shelter from the already blazing sun. To my left I saw a clearing where a substantial landslide had swept away everything in its wake, and a little further I decided to rest beneath the trees. It was so nice to get that backpack off and feel some cool air.

At the top of the ascent, the trail led me across a long, grassy field and back out onto the sun-baked South Downs Way. I turned right to continue my westward course. To the south of the path was a continuous line of trees and to the north was this long meadow of deep green grass, with the trees marking the edge of the escarpment beyond. A cycle race was in progress and bikes continually streaked past me as I continued. The route seemed to continue in this way for a few miles, which suited me as I was relieved to be on flat terrain at last.

The descent to the next valley was spectacular, and being relatively straight, I was able to maintain a significant speed. The A286 at the bottom would mark the end of my jaunt along 'The Way' this time, but we will continue westward to Winchester in a later chapter (South Downs West).

Some marshals were doling out safety advice to the racers and apologised upon realising that I wasn't a participant. However, the advice along the lines of 'don't get killed on the main road' was worth having anyway. I turned left to head southward, and the next few miles along the main road positively breezed by. I eventually descended to the village of Singleton on the southern side of the range of hills.

I made a beeline for the churchyard and left my bike by the gate. I then sat on a wall on the other side of the church and finished my wrap, washing it down with another hefty swig of soft drink. Again, it didn't cross my mind that I might be getting blasé about leaving my velocipede unattended. It was the countryside after all.

My plan was to head for Chichester, maybe get some lunch in a chain pub that I am trying not to promote by name too obviously, and then perhaps explore Selsey Bill (about eight miles beyond the cathedral city and administrative centre of West Sussex). So I continued along the A286 until a lane to the left descended gently into the small valley to enable me to pick up The Centurion Way – a converted railway line that I knew well – a remnant of the line that used to run from Chichester to Midhurst.

I'm not sure if this was the same cycle race or a different one, but more bikes with Lycra-clad riders were zipping by as I neared the brick bridge over the former trackbed. It was here that our routes parted; the cyclists were going up and over while I branched off to the right to join The Centurion Way southward.

All that bitter lemon drink meant that I was now in need of a basic function, so I left my bike against a gate and disappeared beneath the brick bridge and into the thicket beyond (the trackbed to the north of this point is abandoned). As I wandered back from the weedy bank, I realised that this might be the last truly shady and peaceful spot where I could take a rest today, but before I sat down, I thought I'd better check on my bike.

Now this is where it all went weird, as I was about to unravel my chain from around the seat strut in order to secure my bike to the gate when I felt the burn of disapproving eyes. I looked across the field and saw a tractor running up and down ploughing, and wondered if perhaps the farmer disapproved of me blocking an access point with my bike. So in a bizarre moment of confusion, I left my bike unsecured and returned to beneath the bridge to enjoy the briefest of moments in the shade. I could hear the gentle sound of cyclists sporadically passing above me, sometimes accompanied by the encouraging voices of the marshals, but when I returned to the gate I got the shock of my life – no bike!

'No, this can't be!' I thought, 'This must be a prank!' I had experienced this before in the village of Harrietsham in Kent, where I had left my bike unsecured outside the village shop, only to find that kids had moved it a hundred yards up the road when I emerged. Surely this was the worst thing that could happen in the countryside, right?

So I wandered back to where The Centurion Way had departed from the track that goes over the bridge, expecting to find my bike dumped in the hedge there, but there was nothing. The tractor was still traversing the field and the world was continuing exactly as it had been ten minutes before.

What baffled me was that I'd had a sense of somebody watching, but just couldn't place my finger on how this was. I half expected Derren Brown to dive out of the bushes and declare that I had fallen victim to one of his mind experiments and that hopefully this trick will teach me to be more vigilant when it comes to locking up my bike. But there was no Derren and no bike. I would have been happy with either.

All I could do was to begin pounding the five miles back to Chichester on foot, hoping to find my bike abandoned somewhere along the route. I asked a few people if they had seen anybody riding a bike like mine but nobody had. Most of them expressed similar disbelief that such a thing could happen in such a remote location. It was as though somebody had been staked out there all day, just waiting for someone to abandon a bike and pop over the gate for a toilet break. And seriously, how likely is that?

I deduced that the last chance of being reunited with my bike would be right at the end of the route, as it curved slowly round to enter Chichester from the west. Surely it had to be left against a fence-post, perhaps with a polite note saying, 'Many thanks for the ride into the city. Please be more careful in future.'

But yet again my hopes were dashed – there was absolutely nothing. The bike was gone - brown bread, kaput, vanished off the face of the earth, etc. So you see now that when I finally got a replacement bike and would excuse myself to startled ramblers by saying, 'My bell's been stolen,' I wasn't really lying at all. There just happened to be a bike attached to it when it was taken!

I eventually reached the station and grabbed a pricey coffee from the platform café for the journey, but no amount of caffeine would lift my mood or dispel my sense of complete disbelief. My adventure had ended in a shambles and I made the four-hour train journey home in a state of numbness and borderline apathy.

This bike had accompanied me all over Southern England on trip after trip. It had even survived a night at a local pub when itinerant yobs decided it would be fun to remove it from against the wall, drive over it in their (probably stolen) car and then put it back against the wall in a mangled state. But now that this Trojan of a bike was somebody else's, I can only conclude with the obvious joke that as I relieved my bladder in that remote spot, it was the thief who was really taking the micturation.

Wonderful the human race, isn't it?

HAMPSHIRE (TEST VALLEY)

5) Romsey's Royalty

The brilliant thing about this book is that when things go wrong, the next section is always taking place at a previous point in the space-time continuum, so it is now Good Friday and I still have my bike.

The booking office at my local station was closed and I quickly abandoned the idea of getting any sense out of the ticket machine and waited on Platform 2 for the Brighton service.

The two-carriage diesel train was busy as I boarded, and as we traversed the Sussex seaside towns of Rye, Hastings, Bexhill and Eastbourne, the sense of claustrophobia got successively worse. Wedged between a gaggle of students and my bike, I dreaded the next two stops – Polegate and Lewes – because the doors, which were currently jammed up with my non-folding mountain bike, would soon be opening, and people with zero patience would be expecting me to vaporise my bike in order for them to achieve instant access.

On trains, you always feel that if you are in possession of a bike you are some kind of 'untouchable' – a lower class, looked down upon by all and sundry. Even if you have been waiting on the platform for half an hour and the doors open right in front of you, you are expected to hang back and let the 'non bicycle people' board first. The one occasion where the English will quite happily jump a queue is if the person in front has a bike.

That said, I was quite surprised that by the time I reached Brighton, no less that two people had helped me to extricate my rucksack from the mass of human bodies crammed into the carriage like sardines.

Brighton was heaving. It was sunny and it was Easter, so what do you expect? The next train was bound for a place called Woolston. Due to engineering works, it couldn't quite make it to Southampton, but the will was clearly there, as I would only have to revise my route by about a mile.

This train was relatively quiet and the guard was a budding humourist. The announcements were so full of passion that it even prompted the young man opposite me to smile and comment. I have never heard anybody get so excited about stopping at places with names like 'Angmering' in my entire life.

In fact this kind of humour seems to be the norm in this neck of the woods. I recall once before waiting at the station at Shoreham-by-Sea when some bright spark had decided to play the theme music to The Great Escape over the tannoy system, giving passengers a rare opportunity to smile and exchange shy comments to one another. 'Get Britain talking' - maybe that's the strapline of Southern Railway's West Coastway service.

Unfortunately, this train stopped at virtually every conceivable halt along a 65-mile section of coast. By the time I emerged at Woolston, the notion of getting on a bike seemed like freedom incarnate.

With my rucksack on my back, I set off over the toll bridge which crosses the River Itchen near its mouth into Southampton Water. As I gazed southward, the water was blue, as was the sky, and I was prompted to stop and take a photo.

I then cruised down the other side into the docklands of Southampton. I tried to push out my mind the memories that this place conjured up, for I'd had a job for around six years where driving lorry-loads of goods from Kent to the company's cruise-ships at this port was a regular feature. There was nothing bad in this, in fact the free lunch on board ship was a very enjoyable perk, however I wasn't here to be reminded of jobs and the former tribulations of work. I turned my eyes to the other side of the road to admire the city walls. Amazingly I'd never noticed them before.

This dogleg of the A33, which comes down from Reading, Basingstoke and Winchester and takes a 90-degree turn west when it hits the coast, was gradually whipping itself up into something resembling an urban motorway. This was not the kind of road I sought for these rides, and as I neared the pivotal junction with the M271, a waft of air from a nearby McDonald's caused me to cross the roundabout beneath the flyover and pop in for a Quarter Pounder and a searing-hot cup of tea.

Beyond this, I found a lane that effectively bypassed the roundabout with the M271 and led me beneath the road that goes to Totton and the New Forest, to the tranquil banks of the River Test; tranquil, were it not for the rail line next to it. As I passed an industrial estate or two, things got more rural. I could even hear birds. Now I was living the dream!

Before long, my lane had took me beneath the M27, through the small village of Lee and out to the main A-road to Romsey. Being beside a river, it was a nice, flat start to this particular mission. I rode along the footpath beside the road into Romsey and was waved across the carriageway at a busy roundabout by a courteous truck driver. It seemed that there was an outbreak of pleasantness among the sometimes lugubrious English on this particular Good Friday. Fat cats who want to reduce the number of bank holidays from 'not many' to 'hardly any' should take note.

I passed what looked like an Art Deco style cinema and headed for the town centre. Little did I know that there were enough attractions in Romsey to keep me here for a good hour or two.

I chained my bike up near the abbey and was about to wander in when I realised that a service was taking place. I guessed that aimless meandering wouldn't be the most desirable thing, but as soon as I walked away, a lady rushed out with a leaflet and informed me that the service would be over in ten minutes. I was beginning to get used to this courtesy.

Serendipitously, I came across King John's House. This stone building had a wattle and daub medieval cottage tacked to the front of it, but the rear, which to my mind looked a little like a small chapel, indeed dates from the thirteenth century.

I wandered around the little gardens which were beautifully wild. Visitors were asked not to walk on the meadow areas which were a flood of colour – bluebells, anemomes, celandines, primroses, in fact all the classic spring wildflowers. I stopped to admire the gently trickling stream at the back and it was one of those moments when you realise that life is good. And so to the inside.

Today, there was an art exhibition taking place, which meant that entry was free. Hurrah! I asked where the best place to leave my bulky rucksack would be and then perused the two floors. I learned that the name was a bit of a misnomer, for it is now believed that the building could not have been King John's hunting lodge as it dates from around forty years after his death. However, the name had just stuck and was not up for changing.

One thing that grabbed my attention was a section of the original floor under glass which was made of broken bones. It seemed a macabre way to construct a floor and I sent a photo of it to a friend of mine who writes horror novels. One of his tales included a building with walls made out of skulls, but in hindsight it would seem that the builders of the 13th century wouldn't be too shocked by such an idea.

The art was interesting too. There was a bright, impressionist style hillscape and a similar picture of Stonehenge. I wandered upstairs to find some psychedelic style biro drawings, consisting of eyes and swirling patterns. The blurb said that the artist had no idea what the pictures would be like upon commencing, but merely let the pen and the subconscious take the lead and see what emerged. I liked this notion.

A man was talking to a lady called 'Squish', and was using her name as a full stop at the end of every sentence. The furthest room was set up as a banqueting room, complete with a plastic pig's head on a plate.

And so, I emerged, feeling relaxed and edified, and wandered across to the abbey. The interior was as impressive as some cathedrals I had visited. However, I'd only ridden around 12 miles, so it was time to reacquaint myself with my wheels and head northward on the A-road.

After a couple of miles, the Test Way began. This cycle route is part of the National Cycle Network and follows the route of an old railway line to Stockbridge and beyond. To begin with, it hugs the edge of the road. This is of course nicer than riding on the road itself, but the real satisfaction kicks in when the two conduits part company. To my right I could see chalky cliffs where road and former rail line cut through the hills.

About halfway to Stockbridge there is an old station – Horsebridge. It is not compulsory for all place names along the route to end in 'bridge' but it certainly helps.

The station building is behind a hedge as it is now a private residence, but on certain days a tearoom is open and one gets a chance to mooch around the platforms where there were even a few old carriages.

Beyond this, the Test Way bridges the river of the same name, and I stood to admire the view as the waters flowed in a meandering 'S' shape southward. Birds sang loudly and the moment was positively idyllic. I took out my smartphone and filmed a minute of the tranquil scene. My aim was to post it on one of those video sharing sites (we don't advertise for Google here) as a minute of peace. Perhaps anybody, from the stressed office employee to the depressed, spurned lover, could use my short clip as therapy to tranquillise their minds. Or maybe you have to actually be there.

And so to Stockbridge.

The Test Way emerged from the meadow-lands and led out to a roundabout on the A30. Conveniently to the right was a pub. Oh bliss!

But first, I decided to wander along Stockbridge High Street. This was another idyllic scene. The A30 is relatively peaceful at this point, for the A303 usurps it between the M3 and Honiton, leaving the former arterial road for the use of tourist and traveller alike. The High Street in Stockbridge is dead straight, with a hill at each end. The hill to the west was golden with rapeseed, and in the middle of the scene the steeple of the church protrudes above the rooftops.

During the course of this quite long village street, the road bridges various strands of water which seem to have become temporarily detached from the River Test. I remembered wandering beside one of these streams between some houses in my visit to Stockbridge three years before, while learning about the split between two alternative political/social movements from a friend over the phone. It reminded me a little of the People's Front of Judea and Judean People's Front feud in Monty Python's film 'The Life of Brian.'

I scuttled back to the pub and opted for a pint of Seafarer Ale. As I sat outside on a bench, I was pleased to hear authentic West Country accents from the middle-aged customers out for a Good Friday pint (or gallon). I took a photograph of my beer and sent it to my girlfriend and one of my camping buddies with the caption, 'My first outdoor pint this year.' Then I remembered that I'd already been camping once and had consumed considerably more than a pint, so this attempt at smarminess wasn't strictly correct.

After a second pint went down like a snake's foot, it was time to move on, with just a brief visit to the Co-op shop to delay me.

I didn't yet know that the Test Way continued northward from here, but I was jolly pleased that it did. It began by sticking close to the A-road again, but soon found its own course, and the handful of bridges overhead confirmed that I was still on the former railway line.

It was beginning to get a little dusky, which meant that I needed to keep my eyes open for suitable camping sites. I spotted the remains of two diverging platforms at what used to be Fullerton Junction. The one to the right wasn't fenced off and I even toyed with the idea of camping there, but as I continued I was glad that I didn't. It was a little too close to a house and caravan to assure me 100% solitude – essential when camping at an 'unofficial' location.

Just beyond this, I was faced with a choice; a sign pointed one way towards Andover, and another way towards Wherwell claiming it to be 'one of the most picturesque villages of the Test Valley.' I decided that I had to check out this grandiose claim.

My route then led onto a lane, with the former trackbed now upon a disused embankment to my left. The Test was to my right and I stopped to walk across a long wooden bridge which traversed several strands of the picturesque river before crossing a public meadow to Chilbolton.

I returned to the lane and continued. Wherwell did indeed live up to its moniker of 'picturesque.' There was an impressive concentration of thatched roofs here.

My road had become a B-road by now, and beyond the village, I took a wander up onto the railway embankment, to find that there was some kind of path running in the cutting below. However, my aim now was to get into the nearby Harewood Forest, as this seemed my best option for a peaceful night's sleep.

It was a little way before the B-road hit the mighty A303 that I found a turning, northward, into the wood. To begin with, it was a trackway leading past chicken houses with large gas tanks attached. Three deer sprinted across the path, one behind the other, as I rode into the woods. Then a footpath crossed. I later realised that this was part of the Roman road that led from Andover to Winchester, which further south forms the western end of the A272 – a road which has even had a book published about it; not by me I hasten to add (although it is the kind of thing that I just might do).

Another path then diverged, and a little way along this I decided that my best bet was to camp behind a fallen tree on the bank between the two paths. Having laid out my sleeping bag upon my piece of tarpaulin, I broke open the pack of smoked salmon and enjoyed this salty bliss with some raw mushrooms.

And as the skies grew more crepuscular, I settled down into the sleeping bag, still wearing my jacket and augmenting this with a woolly hat. I was expecting a cold night ahead. A deer came within ten feet of me, stood for a while and then disappeared, and then there was just me, the stars up above and the gentle roar of traffic on the A303.

6) Andover Ambience

The dreams conjured up in a sleeping bag in the middle of a forest are always interesting. I remember waking up several times and seeing the constellation of The Plough (Big Dipper if you're from the USA) horizontally overhead. However, on one occasion I thought I'd woken up and found it to be at a perpendicular angle. Logic tells me that this must have been a dream.

In another dream I looked up the bank and saw my old scoutmaster, camping with a group of scouts. What a coincidence that somebody from the same village should choose exactly the same bank in exactly the same forest, out of all the forests in the UK to take his troop!

I got up at 8am. It was so cold that I put on a second jumper beneath my jacket. I donned gloves as well, before commencing my ride. By now, you may be wondering why I don't have a tent. One part of the answer is that I imagine the weight to be too cumbersome for me to enjoy the cycling aspect of these trips carrying a tent on my back. The other part is that I wish to draw as little attention to myself as possible because none of my campsites are 'official.'

It is a sad fact that to officially camp anywhere in the UK you generally have to pay money to somebody who already has more money than you, before you can even think about getting some kip. Meanwhile, the public woodlands are 'public' for just about everything except camping, so as you can see, unless I wish to shell out extra cash, the sleeping part has to be done very surreptitiously, and let's not forget, the aim of these trips is a cheap holiday after all. There are enough other activities in life to haemorrhage money from one's wallet.

And so, with sleeping bag bundled into rucksack and tarpaulin folded up on top, I retraced my route, down the footpath, along the track past the chicken huts, along the B-road through the village of thatched cottages and back to that long, wooden bridge over the River Test. Beyond this bridge, I rode across the meadow to Chilbolton and then turned right, along the lane through the village to arrive back on the Test Way near Fullerton Junction.

This time I took the Andover turning, but soon discovered that the continuation of this western spur of the railway was as inaccessible, if not more so, than the eastern one. A foreboding sign stated that it was private land with no right of way. Instead the signed cycle route leads the rider onto the lane via the hamlet of Fullerton and up a long hill – my first significant climb of the trip.

By the time I reached the top I was boiling. Off came the jacket and the second jumper, the hat and gloves having been removed already. I sat on a grassy bank by the side of the road and finished the smoked salmon, washing this down with a cake I'd packed before leaving.

When I continued, I realised that it actually wasn't so hot after all. The route turned right at a crossroads and descended, and by the time I'd reached bottom of the hill I'd made an executive decision to put my jacket back on.

The lane approached the trackbed once again, but the former railway's course was all on private land now. The village of Goodworth Clatford was very pleasant, and I stopped by the ford which no doubt gave the village the last syllable of its name. A wooden bridge had been constructed over the river for pedestrians and a sign warned that the ford was too deep for vehicles, which raised the question, 'Is it actually a ford then?'

I watched a swan gracefully floating about on the water and wondered what it would be like to have a body shaped like a boat and spend most of your life on a meniscus.

After ten minutes of such musings, I pressed on. Upper Clatford stopped me in my tracks too. Here was an old fashioned red phone box which had long lost its phone. It was now being used as a library for anybody wishing to swap their old books for something they actually wanted to read. I left a small handful of my business cards on the shelf, hoping that some literary talent spotter might live in the vicinity and turn my writing from a leisure project into a career. High hopes. These cards had proven to be far more effective in another arena of life, for one of them had been instrumental in meeting my future wife.

I had got chatting to her at a barbecue in London and was surprised to find her response returned in a Russian accent. Thinking about what might interest a tourist visiting our land, I questioned myself as to what I was most proud about in this country. Of course – the music!

Yes, The Beatles, The Stones, The Kinks, The Who, Pink Floyd, Led Zeppelin, David Bowie, Queen, Oasis, Blur, Radiohead, Arctic Monkeys, etc. all arouse much more pride in me than the names of stuffy old generals and leaders with dubious morals. So our conversation was based around the construct of me naming various classic English bands and her saying whether or not she liked them. Lesson one in 'how to strike up conversations in any language.'

By the end of the afternoon, I decided to hand her one of my cards so that she could have a look at my village website and keep in touch by email. I would eventually suggest coming to the UK again to visit Liverpool – home of the greatest band of all time. No, not Freddie and the Dreamers – and anyway, they were from Manchester!

So the moral of the story is that business cards are good for acquiring every human need except, ironically, business.

Shortly beyond this phone box, my lane passed beneath the formidable A303 and I found myself in suburbia, peddling towards the heart of exotic Andover. When I got a feeling that I had reached the centre (lots of roundabouts being the usual clue), I chained up my bike and set off to explore. I anticipated a 'clone town,' but my findings were slightly higher than my expectations. The River Anton looked quite quaint at the centre of the town and there was a town square with scenes from Andover's history depicted in a circle on the ground.

Unlike my hometown of Ashford, Andover hasn't flung its market out into the suburbs like some kind of disgraced schoolboy, but it is right there in the centre where it belongs. Yes, the logical place, where people walk about and might just pop into a few shops and spend a little money rather than jump in their cars and steam off at sixty miles per hour muttering, "What a waste of time that was!"

I found a pub-stroke-hotel and immediately ordered the two things you crave most when you've been sleeping in a wood - a pot of tea and a 'full English' breakfast. I offered the landlord £1 if I could plug my phone in but he said I could charge it for free. Good stuff!

Smartphones are amazing things. You can instantly access a map showing routes you might wish to ride instead of the A303, you can take photographs of pints of English ale to torment your girlfriend in Moscow with, you can even make calls on them, but the one thing that I've never understood is the brevity of the battery life. All that technology, yet a battery that lasts more than a day seems to be a major 'no-no.'

I had purchased a plug-in gadget that can be charged indoors and then plugged into a smartphone later to decant its latent energy, but all in all, this still gives me a maximum of two days usage before I am cut off from all humanity. Ok, the answer is to buy another one of these gadgets perhaps, but how about a phone with a slightly heavier battery for those who enjoy camping or frequenting places away from mains sockets? I'm sure there's a market for it.

I felt relaxed, with cup of tea in hand and phone charging from the wall socket next to me. I usually use this 'pub time' to update my diary and peruse the map – a kind of glimpse into both the past and the future. The breakfast arrived and glided down as though it was on a sea of velvet. Then I ordered a second pot of tea.

Before I left the pub there was one more thing to do. I visited the gents to refill my water-bottle from the tap (not the toilet!) and have a quick 'face and hand-wash.' Oh yes, and use the toilet, but I think the quality of the book will be improved if I don't detail every single aspect of my adventures. However, I left realising that I had forgotten to bring some toothpaste.

After the inevitable visit to Boots I decided to entrust my phone to a market stallholder to replace the broken back panel. That's another thing about smartphones – they're so flaming fragile – one slip onto a tiled floor and they resemble a stained glass window.

As I walked away, I dodged an assertive gypsy woman of the 'you *will* have one of my posies' variety. Then, reunited with my bike, I headed east, eventually finding London Road, which was once part of the A30, which as you'll remember now runs further south via Stockbridge, with the mighty A303 now acting as the major route to the South-West.

The road presented me with a steady climb towards Andover Down. I turned right at the top and followed the lane back into the forest. After around ten miles of riding, I was now a matter of furlongs away from where I'd first opened my eyes that morning.

The lane led me down to the village of Middleton and I found myself in a bit of a funk, with the stiff head-wind forcing me to contemplate a change of route. Plan A was to continue north-east along the Test Valley to its source near Overton and then head towards Basingstoke, picking up the towpath of the Basingstoke Canal which would lead me to the heady delights of Woking. Plan B was to backtrack a little and pick up the Roman road to Winchester, through all its incarnations as a track, a lane, the A272 and finally a B-road into the heart of the city.

I crossed the river and opted for Plan A, at least to begin with. The Test had surprised me in being a picturesque river at virtually every location I had crossed it. I wanted more of this.

This lane had other ideas though, and soon began climbing steeply, before descending to pass beneath the A34 – a monster of a road that is dualled all the way from Winchester to north of Oxford. This is the kind of road that you wouldn't cycle on unless you had a death wish. In truth this mighty highway used to run all the way to Manchester via Birmingham, until some bright spark decided to cunningly disguise most of the Oxford to Birmingham stretch as the A3400. You'd never guess, would you?

We will encounter a lot of this on our travels. If a road gets too big for its boots, the middle section will be duly culled and redesignated. Thus, Britain's road network will make even less sense to a visiting alien than it did before. I guess these Machiavellian disguises protect us from awful truths such as knowing that the A34 runs from Winchester to Manchester. You want the truth? You can't handle the truth!

Anyway, my lane was now much wider than before and seemed to be the original route of the A34, leading me north into the large village of Whitchurch. After being battered by a head-wind for a few miles, it didn't take a lot to entice me out of the saddle. I spotted a newsagent, and the thought of a chocolate milkshake (or 'Yuk drink' for those familiar with my parlance) seemed like nirvana.

Keen to change direction and get out of the wind, I asked a man if there was a track parallel to the southbound A34 that I could use to get to Sutton Scotney (and ultimately Winchester). He suggested climbing over the fence and riding along the edge of the fields. This seemed a bit sketchy to me, so I stoically pressed on, into the village centre and back onto the B-road that used to be the A30 (all these roads changing their names reminded me of 'The Artist Formerly Known As Prince' who eventually reduced himself to an unpronounceable symbol. Ouch!).

Two things grabbed my attention on this four-mile sprint, which approximated the route of The Test but with added hills. The first was a pub called The Watership Down Inn. It was a clever piece of marketing as it was formerly known as The Freefolk Arms ('Prince syndrome' again). However, it did alert me to the fact that the rabbit cartoon that gave Art Garfunkel his second solo number one with 'Bright Eyes' was actually a few miles to the north of this inn. And while we're at it, I think we have to give Mike Batt a mention as the writer of the song, as well as founder of The Wombles pop act and discoverer of Katie Melua.

The second thing that I stopped for was to admire a long terrace of houses, which looked like council / 'housing association' properties but with wonderful thatched roofs.

The next village was Overton - another substantial settlement with a good range of amenities. As I passed the central crossroads, a car was waiting at the lights with Pink Floyd's 'Great Gig in the Sky' blasting out from the windows. I felt that tinge of Great British pride again and almost complimented the driver on his choice, but just managed to rein myself in. Indeed, most music heard emanating from cars tends to be of the computer generated 'soulless' variety, so to hear such a fine piece of existential creativity even for a few seconds was enough to give me an added boost.

So I branched to the left and reacquainted myself with the River Test which was now little more than a stream, in spite of spawning several small lakes in the area. A bridleway took me around the lakes, and as I sat on a bridge by the lane I asked an elderly gent what the chances of locating the source of the river were. His answer was a bit vague, so there was only one thing for it. You've guessed it – the pub.

As I reclined at the bar with a pint of ale from a local brewery, I asked the landlord / barman about locating the source of the river. He explained that due to recent rainfall it had actually moved about a mile further east, as you could see the water flowing through the fields way beyond the spring that is supposed to be The Test's nadir.

Then a man, at a guess in his late sixties, struck up a conversation. He informed me that the paper that is used to make all British money is produced near to the village. He apologised for holding his much younger girlfriend's hand, but I said it was nice to see some romance (instead of Eastenders-style arguing). As he was from Basingstoke I decided to do a little research.

"Is it a new town?" I ventured, "A bit Milton Keynes-ish?"

He explained that although it had increased in size vastly since the sixties it was actually a much older town. When I asked him to estimate the population he replied, "A million and a half." I took this as a joke.

Later a discussion about football broke out. It is not a subject I have any passion for, although having a friend who goes into a three-day depression whenever Arsenal lose a match, I am curious to observe football fans from an anthropological point of view. After two and half pints, it was surely time for more biking.

I now headed south, up a long gentle incline along the road signed 'Micheldever' (I was told that it rhymes with 'never,' not 'diva'). As is often the case after a pint or two I struggled to locate my position on the map. I showed it to a man walking a dog who informed me that he was dyslexic. However, his directions onto a bridleway which would eventually lead me back to the Micheldever road were spot-on.

The lane had some challenging climbs, although at a glance the scenery wasn't particularly dramatic. Micheldever was another quaint little place with thatch in abundance. And soon I hit the A33, which at this point was in 'Roman mode,' being a dead straight conduit from just south of Basingstoke to Winchester. Note, this is a different Roman road to the A272 one I mentioned earlier, in fact these historic, dead straight routes fan out from Winchester in most conceivable directions.

'The Romans didn't mess about,' I thought, as I tackled the inclines. They didn't deviate roads around hills, generally going right up over the top.

And so, it was with some relief that I drew near to the former capital of England. In the interest of nostalgia, I decided to cut through to Abbots Worthy and pick up the footpath along the River Itchen. I had walked this riverside trail into Winchester back in 2006 on that epic walk to Somerset with my friend Tom. To reach it, I dismounted as a mark of respect while passing in front of a private house, beyond which I ignored the 'no cycling' signs as usual. If there's nobody about to get offended, I can't see the harm.

It was where the track passed under the A33 that it all went a bit 'Pete Tong' (he's been honoured with an MBE now so please show some respect when using this phrase). The recent flood had rendered the path beyond a quagmire. I'd had enough wet-footed, brown-shoed experiences in the past to know that the most sensible thing to do in this situation is a U-turn. 'You turn if you want to,' spoke Margaret Thatcher. OK, I will.

So, it was up onto the pavement beside the A34, all the way to the roundabout, which had no means for pedestrians to cross other than to run like hell in front of the speeding traffic. I soon located the centre of Winchester and navigated my way to the nearest Wetherspoons pub. I fancied a curry.

A man at the bar was supping a bright green liquid from a pint glass. I elicited some words from myself along the lines of, "What on earth is that?" The enterprising barman quickly poured me a sample and I found that it tasted just like normal bitter.

"I'll try a half," I tentatively replied.

Sitting down at a nearby table, I supped the Stonehenge Ale, as it was called, and awaited the chicken tikka masala. The gent from the bar asked how I was finding the green ale as he passed me.

"It tastes just like normal beer!" I replied.

Well, it's certainly a talking point and anything that gets the shy, reserved English talking to each other has got to be a good thing in my book. Meanwhile, the curry went down like... well, you know what I mean – *'le pied de serpent'* as they might say in France if they were silly enough.

There was just time to say I'd seen the cathedral before my journey continued. Obviously I'd been to Winchester several times before, but I think in these provincial cities, I find it much harder to tick all the boxes on the 'must visit' list as I pass through than in the smaller settlements. For example, I could say 'I've done Romsey,' but could I really say 'I've done Winchester' on any of my visits? I'm not sure.

I picked up the path beside the river and there were some substantial hills to my left as I rode away from the city, southward. After a while I noticed that the waterway next to me was not at the bottom of the valley and deduced that this was a 'navigation' parallel to the River Itchen.

The path eventually became a proper cycle route and took me over a long viaduct bridge, which trains had once thundered across. The mighty M3 roared away to the east of me as it ripped its way up through Twyford Down, the scene of many a pitched battle at the time of its construction. The capitalists v the environmentalists.

My aim was to head for Twyford village, and I decided to follow the blue 'cycle way' signs, which took me up a road, which clearly used to be the A33 before the M3 rendered it obsolete, and then down a lane to the hamlet of Shawford. Dusk was falling and I shot off into a little parkland area to see if there were any suitable camping spots, but the constant drone of the M3 on the hillside above would have made sleep something of a luxury, so I returned to the road by cycling along the Itchen Navigation. I then followed the lane through green meadows to Twyford.

The final few miles were due south, until a footpath enticed me away from the B-road. The wood felt more like a wild area at the end of somebody's back garden, so I descended to a lane across the field beyond, and after another one of those indecisive funks riding up and down the lane, I streaked off up a bridleway passing horse pastures. It reached a crossroads of paths at the corner of a wood. Up the bank I spotted a fallen tree and thus, my spot was chosen. Down went the tarp and the sleeping bag, up went a few disguising branches and into the sleeping bag went the cyclist.

A disco was pumping away somewhere nearby. I could hear children's voices and when these had subsided a dog began to bark. It was actually more of a shout than a bark.

'What is the point of that?' I thought to myself, wishing it would just shut up. The wind rustled the tall, spindly trees overhead, and I pushed concerns about them toppling over out of my head as consciousness slowly ebbed away for another night.

7) Wet in 'Waltham'

The dream that my mind had concocted that night illustrated my repressed fear of being found by unwelcoming (and unwitting) hosts. A crowd of people were standing around my camping spot and I asked, "Are you going to call the police?" The reply was 'Yes,' but when the boys in blue arrived I was unconcerned, as I suddenly realised that it was a dream.

This phenomenon is known as 'lucid dreaming' and it is possible to use it to your advantage and control the dream. However, I find that more often than not it works the other way round; dreams seem to have a subconscious influence on our actions.

Often I find myself visiting some obscure place I haven't been to for years, suddenly realising that I dreamed about it the night before. Or perhaps I find myself getting unusually angry about something (perhaps a phone box in Farnborough?), mirroring similar emotions to those I felt in a dream.

Anyway, I awoke hearing a sound that resembled raindrops falling on a tarpaulin. I quickly shuffled things around so that I could cover myself with the sheet ready for the downpour, but then I realised that it was not the pitter-patter of rain but a crackling of leaves which occurred every time a gust of wind passed through the wood.

It wasn't until a real drop of water hit my face at 7.30am that I decided now was the time to pack up and head out. The sky was now overcast and it seemed that I'd seen the best of the weather for this Easter break. My aim was to get to the South Coast from where I could easily get a train home if required.

With backpack in tow, I marched off up the wooded, southbound bridleway and emerged onto a lane which passed Marwell Zoo. Maybe the 'shouting dog' had been something more wild.

I then came out onto the former Portsmouth to Winchester road and headed east, in the direction of Bishop's Waltham. This was quite a wide B-road, with a few undulations, and upon reaching the town, I went in search of tea and sustenance.

On Easter Sunday morning, the centre was something of a ghost town. People were walking dutifully up the picturesque alleyway leading to the church as the bells pealed out their summons. I struggled to find a pub or a reasonably priced breakfast, so I relented and ventured into a branch of Costa. It was pleasant enough and I enjoyed a *croque-monsieur* at a table at the back of the café. The 'lavs' performed the usual threefold function and then I decided it was time to look at the remains of the palace. The ruins date from the twelfth and fourteenth centuries, and the palace was destroyed by order of Oliver Cromwell in 1644. However this stone 'skeleton' with its numerous plaques informing the visitor as to the purpose of each room is well worth a visit.

The skies now looked angry and a hazy drizzle was threatening, so it was back to the bike and onward to the next large village – Wickham. I had been here before when cycling the disused rail line down from West Meon, but I couldn't recall the large village square, which gives me some concern as to the level of accuracy I am going to be able to summon when I come to write up the earlier trips in this book.

There are five disused rail lines which run up from the South Coast due north that can now be used by cyclists. You should be getting used to a few of their names by now. The westernmost is the Test Way that I rode via Stockbridge. Moving east, the next is this Meon Valley Trail. Then there is the Centurion Way from Chichester towards Singleton (the remains of the Midhurst line), the Downs Link from Shoreham-by-Sea up towards Horsham and ultimately Guildford, and finally there's the Cuckoo Trail from Polegate in East Sussex up to Heathfield.

From Wickham I knuckled under for a long climb on the busy A32, which was resplendent with a 'crawler lane.' There was a long freewheel down to Fareham, passing beneath the M27. My original plan was to branch off before this descent and follow the lanes along the top of the hills above Portchester, but the incessant drizzle meant that I was all but ready to throw the towel in. Then, as I made my way to the railway station the skies just opened. I dived for cover in the nearest church doorway and waited for the shower to pass. The weather had proclaimed that this particular adventure was now at a close. I headed for the train station and lobbed in my metaphorical towel.

The rail journey home was something of an epic, with maintenance work breaking out like a rash across the network. Rail replacement buses are all well and good until you try to get on one with a pushbike. In spite of there being a large storage area underneath most coaches, the official policy is 'no bikes,' galvanising my view about the cyclist being a second class customer on the rails.

So my route home was like the drunken man's stagger, zigzagging inland and back to the coast, involving five trains, six hours and two pubs. The first one, near Redhill station, was serving Speckled Gold ale in bottles for £1.99. I savoured both the price and the beer as spectators cheered at the Arsenal v Hull game on the big screens. I was assured by the snatches I caught that my Arsenal supporting friend would not be plagued by the black dog that night. The second pub was a pit-stop for a swift half in Tonbridge.

And so with another trip complete, we now have to delve back a little further. This time, we're heading for The Chilterns.

THE CHILTERNS (RIDGEWAY EAST)

8) Wendover Wash-out

We are now going to rewind to the previous autumn; September to be precise. I knew little about The Chiltern Hills before this journey, other than that they seem quite scenic when travelling through the massive cutting on the M40. My 1985 edition of the Guinness Book of Answers informs me that at 45 miles in length, they form England's sixth largest hill range (after the Pennines, North Downs, Cotswolds, South Downs and Cheviots). I imagine that this pecking order hasn't changed in the proceeding thirty years. Not even a Tory MP can successfully apply cuts to a hill range.

I caught the bullet train into London St Pancras from Ashford. Please note that there is no 'e' in this station's name, as is often misquoted, unlike those other well known London termini, St Liver, St Kidney and St Uterus.

It was then a quick pedal along London's inner ring road to Euston to catch my ongoing train to the Hertfordshire town of Tring. Alighting in the early afternoon, I headed north-west along a lane that brought me to a B-road, marked on my map as the Icknield Way.

"What on earth is that?" I hear you ask.

Well, it's an ancient route that connected Wiltshire with Norfolk. Some of it coincides with The Ridgeway so it shares the epithet 'Britain's oldest road' (more about this later). In this particular area it splits into two parallel strands – upper and lower. I duly turned left, although the historical vibes eluded me, and began my journey along the ridge of The Chilterns.

Parallel to this road was a branch of the Grand Union Canal, which once linked the little town of Wendover to the mighty conduit which runs from London into the Midlands. I found a lane that took me down to a bridge over this now-redundant stub, and immediately began cycling the grassy towpath.

The perils of cycling on grass are something I've learned the hard way. Possessing a reasonably robust mountain bike, I would never have imagined the damage that a few stubborn blades can cause to the gears if they become entangled. Several times I have known them to completely pull off part of the mechanism, rendering the bike useless and curtailing many an enjoyable day out. Today I was lucky.

On my map, I noticed a section where the canal seemed to go missing. I had assumed that this was where it plunged into a tunnel. However, to my surprise it just suddenly ended as I rounded a curve in its course. The middle few miles had been blocked up and I believe there are now plans to reunite the two estranged sections.

For me, this meant heading back to the last bridge and then up to the B-road, a.k.a. the Upper Icknield Way, which now presented me with a sustained climb up to a bridge over the A41, marking my entry into Buckinghamshire. Looking to my right as I crossed, the view of this dual carriageway ripping through the hillside and cascading down onto the panorama of farmland below was quite dramatic.

The A41 used to be the UK's tenth longest road (London to Birkenhead), but when the M40 was extended, the middle section was cunningly renumbered as the B4100 to deter through traffic, so like many of Britain's long distance routes, the A41 now consists of two completely unrelated sections of road. I suppose it suffers from a similar situation as the canal – a bit like that magic trick where you saw the woman in half and then separate the two halves.

It was then time for me to descend off of the hills, using the road that had presumably been the A41 in the days before such a strident upgrade was needed.

I searched for the southernmost half of the canal at the bottom of the hill, but somehow missed the bridge and ended up in the village of Aston Clinton. I then took a narrow lane which climbed steeply to a hump-back bridge and thus found myself by the tranquil waterway, heading south-west once again.

The towpath was more conducive to cycling on this section, being a solid surface, although in places the canal seemed pretty narrow and overgrown with weeds. There were some nice, shady curves beneath the arching trees, and all in all I found this to be a picturesque little jaunt.

At Wendover I was convinced that the canal should come to a more conclusive finish, but as I looked along various residential roads to see if there was a way to access a continuation of the towpath, I soon realised that that was it – *finito* - so I thought I'd have a look at Wendover instead.

I rounded a sharp corner into the main, climbing, central shopping street, and it would have been a pleasant place to stop for a pint, but I forced myself to keep on riding. So after what can only be described as a glimpse of the town, I did a U-turn and headed back the way I came, eventually finding a lane which took me underneath the A413.

This led me to a B-road, which was part of the Lower Icknield Way, and apart from a short section where an A-road steals its thunder, this B4009 runs along the bottom of The Chiltern Hills all the way to Wallingford in Oxfordshire.

As I rode, I caught a fleeting glimpse of the Chiltern Brewery on my left-hand-side. Around a hundred yards after passing the entrance, brain processes had correctly interpreted the information and I found myself doing a U-turn. The lure of a pint of artisanal bitter had proven too much, just as the lure of getting the word 'artisanal' in is proving too much now.

From the outside it looked like a shed, but inside I found a very pleasant shop selling all kinds of bottled ales, and if my memory serves me well, there were four different ales on tap to enjoy by the glass. I tried two of these and can confirm that the Chiltern Gold was particularly lively and refreshing. Business was pretty lively too, with all the outdoor chairs occupied by customers, so I initially sat on a stile in the corner of the field to quaff my purchase.

Fighting the desire to try all four beers, I mounted my trusty steed again and continued along the road. A rude awakening followed, as once I reached the A-road section that I mentioned just now, a moronic lorry driver rammed on his horn aggressively, almost propelling me from the bicycle seat in shock. I'm not sure what message this was intended to communicate. Perhaps he misunderstood the law and thought that cyclists have no right to use major routes. Maybe he thought he was doing me a favour and alerting me to the fact that his driving was so poor that I might have to leave the road in order to escape certain death. I'm not sure, but the sport of 'bike scaring' unfortunately seems to be on the rise.

On the local roads near to my home at this time, I often found myself on the receiving end of this from the driver of a small, white hatchback. This used to scare the living daylights out of me as I cycled to a nearby pub on dark, autumn evenings. One feels vulnerable enough on a bleak, country road at night, but when a horn is blasted at you continuously for several seconds, the first thought that arises is getting off the road to avoid decapitation. The car then passes with its occupants laughing at the merriment they have caused, while you are left standing at the side of the road, with a pounding heart and a head full of rude words.

Another more inventive practitioner of the 'sport' once decided to unscrew the lid on a plastic bottle of drink and then throw it into my front wheel, so that the lid flew off and the contents sprayed out. Whilst I admire his ingenuity, I wonder was it really worth spending in excess of a pound on a bottle of Lucozade just to achieve this effect?

It was a far more ominous kind soaking that I was worried about now, for as I headed south-west, the skies ahead looked dark and angry, thunder rumbled in the distance and lightning was flashing sporadically up on the hills ahead.

I reached a pivotal crossroads and immediately decided to branch left towards the nearest town – Princes Risborough. The skies then opened. I flung the bike down onto the grass verge, pulled the tarpaulin from my rucksack and then covered both myself and the bike. It was a surreal experience to be cocooned in a blue womb by the side of the road. The pounding of rain was deafening, and when I glanced out from underneath the bright blue cover I could see why – the grass was covered in little golf balls – I was caught in a hailstorm.

I must have laid there by the side of the road waiting for the deluge to subside for around 20 minutes. I then tentatively emerged and continued my ride into Princes Risborough, but this reprieve proved to be giving me a false sense of security. The rain began to lash down again, and I recall pedalling faster as the water sprayed up from my tyres in a constant leg-soaking jetty. This was far worse than a few splashes from an itinerant bottle of Lucozade.

I pummelled my way onward, beneath a railway bridge and then dived for cover in the porchway of a little police station. In this soaked state, I decided to attempt to make a Skype call to my girlfriend in Moscow to illustrate the changeability of the British climate. All the call really illustrated was the British obsession with the weather, as I kept being distracted by assessing the skies in hope that they would lighten. Like a bird poking its beak out of the nest, I eventually wandered out from the doorway to continue my retreat back to civilisation – Tesco's!

I made a beeline for the toilets and used the blowers to try to dry various areas of my clothing by lifting my legs or holding various sections of my coat beneath the monodirectional gust of warm air. This seemed to take around 15 minutes, with several bewildered people wandering in and out, wondering what on earth I was doing.

After having burned about a megawatt of electricity, I felt obliged to make a purchase. Well, I was hungry anyway if the truth be known. I emerged from the store with a 'bargain' selection of sushi rolls, although admittedly these never taste quite the same when bought from a supermarket.

The town seemed quite pleasant, being that optimum size where it is large enough to have a good range of town centre shops, cafés, etc. but it hasn't quite reached the stage where the clone shops move in and the out of town estates go up, leaving the town centre looking like a ravaged hulk where even the 99p shops can no longer compete because a 98p shop has just opened in the store formerly known as Woolworths.

There is a nice clock tower on an island at the centre of the town that you can walk about beneath. I would discover that these are something of a feature in these small Chiltern towns.

At this stage, I still had time to catch a train home and be safely tucked up in bed by midnight, but I think I'd already decided to commit to camping in spite of the meteorological inclemency, so I headed southward and put my mind to the task of finding my way onto The Ridgeway.

At over 5,000 years old The Ridgeway is reputedly the oldest road in Britain, running for 87 miles from Overton Hill in Wiltshire to Ivinghoe Beacon in Buckinghamshire, which is around five miles north-east of Tring. The Ridgeway crosses the River Thames at Goring, which is roughly the halfway point. To the west of this, it is a substantial track that can be used by horses, cyclists and other 'undesirables,' whereas to the east, it is predominantly designated 'footpath.' I had done my research though, and knew of a substantial rideable section from just south of Princes Risborough to just south of Watlington.

At this point in time I was struggling to find it though. I rode along the lanes to the south of Princes Risborough, but every time I encountered the track it was in 'footpath mode.' I even cycled needlessly up a long hill along a lane, climbing right up onto the ridge, only to realise that the access point was back near the bottom, and you can guess what the trail did as soon as I'd located it. That's right – it climbed straight back up to the top.

What goes up must come down, and my route descended through woodlands to settle into position, running along the bottom portion of the ridge. It was at this point I began to feel at home, for it resembled our own Pilgrim's Way in Kent, another ancient trackway which bumps its way along the bottom of the North Downs on a series of lanes and byways. It was good to be surrounded by trees as well, for this meant that finding a camping spot would be relatively easy. I sat on a bank munching my pseudo-sushi as the light began to fade.

At the next junction of paths I bore left to climb a little and found an area of flat ground in which to lay out the tarp which had proven so valuable in that hailstorm earlier. With my sleeping bag on top, and rucksack as always doing service as a makeshift pillow, I decided to go for a wander.

I followed the footpath all the way to the top of the ridge where it eventually became a lane servicing a few isolated dwellings. I turned around, and as I descended back into the forest, this enhanced the sensation of darkness falling, for with no torch, the dusk felt so thick you could feel it. I made my way back to the 'bedroom' and climbed into the sack.

But this peace was short-lived. I could hear a tree creaking in the gentle breeze, and having seen what a fallen tree can do at the regular camping spot I go to with friends, I decided that half a ton of birch landing on me in the night was not desirable. I picked up all my belongings and moved about ten yards, away from the precarious trunk.

You could say that I partake in two distinct types of camping. The kind indulged in on these rides is what I call 'back to basics' - no tent, no fires, no fixed place to camp and no beer. Whilst the kind of camping I do with friends is comparatively decadent; 'glamping' if you like. Having been given free access to a private woodland by an elderly couple, the four of us pretty much think of it as a second home – a Utopian grotto where anything goes.

Like The Beatles, The A-team and the household in the TV comedy Father Ted, there are four unique characters that seem to operate in synthesis.

The elder of the two brothers is the general master of ceremonies as well as something of a master chef, managing to conjure up all kinds of dishes over a wood-fire. We generally refer to him as 'the godfather' of the camping family, setting everything up, making sure everybody is fed and even looking after the casualties if they seem a bit worse for wear.

The younger brother has a different approach, preferring to lounge in the chair, swigging back can after can of beer and vowing not to get involved in such activities as cooking with the catch-all phrase, 'I don't have the brains to take the reins.' He will occasionally chide anybody not drinking heartily with the phrase, 'You wanna man up a bit,' and generally tries to emulate the lives of the rock band, Kings of Leon. I imagine if he was being savaged by a wild boar his first thought would be, 'What would the Kings of Leon do?' and his second thought would be, 'I'm losing drinking time here!'

Meanwhile, the 'baby' of the camping family has since moved to Norfolk and is now a budding horror-book writer. Perhaps his fascination for the genre could have even been fostered by the traditional notion of scary stories around the campfire. His ever-optimistic outlook can be summed up by his repeated use of the rhetorical phrase, 'How good is that?' I imagine if *he* was being savaged by a wild boar he would say something like, 'Wow - a wild boar – how good is that?'

As for me, I think I started to appreciate camping for its therapeutic qualities - the peaceful sound of birdsong, the gentle breezes rustling the leaves, the warm sunlight streaming into the glade by day and the hypnotic effect of staring into the red embers of the fire by night. However, the conversation will usually at some point prompt me into an impassioned invective aimed at politicians and 'fat cats,' pretty much in the same vein as writing a travel book does. If I was being savaged by a wild boar, I'd probably blame the Government for cuts to fencing subsidies or something similar.

None of the other three have been brave enough to try the 'back to basics' style camp as yet, although it is sometimes talked about. I imagine if they did, the ratio of miles cycled to pub stops would swing dramatically in favour of the latter.

"Don't you get lonely, scared or bored on your own in the wood?" a lot of people ask.

The answer is an unflinching 'no.' The idea of being alone in a big city seems far more isolating to me. I have yet to experience a stranger striking up a conversation in a pub in London, while the scariest thing prowling the wood at night is usually a badger or a fox. Actually, I tell a lie, I did see a wild boar once, but let's build up the anticipation a bit before I get to sharing that experience.

9) 'Murder' in Wallingford

A new day dawned, and as ever after some relaxation, laying in the sleeping bag and taking in the vibes, I extricated myself and bundled it into the rucksack to continue on my merry way.

The Ridgeway became quite rough as the woodland ended and the scenery opened out into green fields. It was a wide, grassy trail with ridges cut into it. I passed many cyclists as I rode, occasionally stopping to munch a few olives from an Italian selection I'd bought in the washroom-cum-superstore yesterday.

Being perhaps a quarter of the way up the hillside, the view to my right was very scenic, and soon the tranquillity was broken by the steadily rising roar of the M40. As I passed beneath it, I recalled the outrage by environmentalists when the M3 was pummelled through Twyford Down near Winchester, and I wondered if there had been a similar furore when this particular section of the M40 was built. It's one hell of a cutting after all! Although being a much older section of motorway, perhaps this construction took place in an era before environmental concerns were prominent in our minds.

Maybe one of the earliest expressions of 'green' sentiment was in 1968 when The Kinks recorded their 'Village Green Preservation Society' album. In 1970, Joni Mitchell echoed the sentiment from across the pond in the lyrics of 'Big Yellow Taxi.' And let's not forget the Teesside folk singer Vin Garbutt with his song 'Photographic Memory' – "If they take away the fields I love then nothing will be left for me to photograph..."

It seems that so often songwriters are ahead of the game in expressing the obvious concerns that politicians would rather hide from the masses in order to keep making all that lovely loot. As mentioned earlier, the battlefield seems to have moved out of the arena of transport and into the area of energy production, with 'fracking' being a particularly hot potato.

Sadly, on occasion the altruistic message is lost, as certain areas of the green movement can be easily hijacked by those who are mainly motivated by keeping the value of their four-bedroom dwellings stratospheric, in objecting to renewable solutions such as wind farms or solar panels while feigning concern for everything from birds to tadpoles. Arguments against renewables often include the hypothesis that the creation of wind farms etc. uses more fossil fuel energy than is saved during their lifetime (let's see some figures please), and also that they are simply uneconomical (figures again please).

I guess the economical argument is down to the sad fact that our politicians choose to invest our money and talent in other areas that are more lucrative, such as flogging weapons to countries we will then fight in ten years time to stop them being used. Most of our MPs seem completely oblivious to the absolute absurdity of this, simply claiming, "It's British jobs on the line."

As the roar receded back into birdsong, The Ridgeway suddenly decided it had had enough of cyclists and dived off up the hillside as a footpath. The trail continued ahead though, now named Swan's Way (reminiscent of Proust?). You can consider that last remark to be the author's in-joke, as it's always good to chuck in a high-brow literary reference to a book you've never read from time to time.

Now, when the off-road trail finally gave up the ghost, a lane took over the course ahead. It was around 100 yards onto the tarmacadam that I realised something was missing – my map! In fact, not just that, but my diary had gone for a burton too, and without these vital notes there could be no book on my adventures.

I retraced my route back onto the trail and up the wooded incline I had just descended, and there on the ground were both. I breathed a sigh of relief and continued.

The lane presented me with a climb and I thought about heading into Wallingford for the customary fry-up, but in the end I decided to press on southward via the undulating, shady village of Ipsden, taking a right turn just beyond to cross the A-road and follow the lanes across the flat, open farmland between the rolling hills. The sky was in that changeable phase where the shadows of clouds on the fields are occasionally broken with sunshine, giving the greens a lighter, more vivid hue.

Another sustained climb awaited me. I remember passing a field covered with small huts and a rather attractive female cyclist. The scenery was pleasant, but by the time I reached Goring, I was gasping for refreshment. I used a back-lane close to the River Thames to reach the centre and headed for a pub that was familiar to me from an earlier visit.

Being a desirable location along the River Thames, popular with the yachting fraternity, I wasn't expecting any bargains, but I must admit to being slightly taken aback by the price of a 'full English' so I opted for the 'posh' breakfast choice instead, this consisting of smoked haddock and a poached egg. It was very tasty, but a second egg wouldn't have gone amiss.

When I emerged, a light shower was beginning to ensue. I wandered along to the long bridges over The Thames and saw that the water was stippled with spots as the rain was hitting the surface. The southward view along the river towards Reading and London is particularly pleasant, with the wooded hills giving the impression that Britain's second longest river has carved itself a gorge, a bit like those photographs of The Rhine you always see in holiday brochures.

I took a little wander along the Thames Path northward from the bridges. It ran past a large hotel complex and eventually made its way to the riverbank. At one of the swing gates a smartly dressed couple were being photographed for some kind of portfolio. A little further I encountered a stall with some crab apples. I can't remember if they were of the 'help yourself' variety or the 'nominal cost' type, but either way, I munched four and then returned to the large hotel to indulge in a beverage while the weather made up its mind.

I then received a phone call, so I wandered out to the decking to provide my counselling service with a modicum of privacy. This tortured soul was in mental turmoil over a relationship which has since finished. Invoking one of the options on the game show 'Who Wants to be a Millionaire,' we'll call him my 'phone a friend' friend. The second call was from a more politicised friend and involved British companies, chemical weapons and Syria. No further comment needed.

After this telephonic interlude, I headed back to my bike and decided to press on along the Thames Path. I had ridden most of this epic trail between London and Goring before, so I was curious as to how it progressed from here. I rode past the crab apple stall again and some very expensive looking dwellings. Sometimes it was a narrow, brown path, while other times it was just the edge of a neatly mown meadow. Either way, I shouldn't have been on it, but riding on the occasional footpath seems a relatively minor indiscretion in the great scheme of things. Let's face it, you're not hearing headlines along the lines of, 'Kent Man Cycles on Thames Path' on the Ten O'clock News.

Eventually the route diverged away from the riverbank and up to the A329. I counted my blessings that nobody had moaned at me for cycling on the footpath and decided to stay on the main road all the way to Wallingford. I made one quick stop in a filling station for a samosa and a cream cake.

And so to Wallingford, which was in Berkshire until 1974, when it swapped its allegiance to Oxfordshire. It has a central market square with an information board. Here I learned that the little town doubles as Causton in the TV drama Midsummer

Murders. I immediately messaged my mum, who is a huge fan of the series. She replied saying that she'd always wanted to visit that town.

I also learned that a Saxon lord had allowed William the Conqueror's invading armies to cross the River Thames here in 1066. As a 'thank you' the town's market traders were allowed to stay open for one extra hour in the evenings. Wallingford also has a castle which was built soon after this. It is just ruins today as its destruction was ordered by Oliver Cromwell.

Much as it was tempting to find a pub and dive in, I felt that I hadn't yet covered enough miles, so I found my way down to the river on the east side of the town centre and continued northward along the Thames Path.

The castle can be seen to the west of the river as you leave the town. I'm not sure that I completely did the place justice, but by now I was on a mission. I crossed a long footbridge over a weir to the village of Benson, where I glimpsed a picturesque little inlet. I then decided to ride the B4009 all the way back to Princes Risborough area, my logic being that if there was a downpour, I could use the return part of my train ticket if I made it as far as Tring. The Chiltern Hills were now running parallel to my right, a couple of miles away.

I had left The Thames to wend its way via Abingdon (where the band Radiohead originate from) and Oxford, where the murders are solved by Inspector Morse rather than DCI Barnaby.

After around seven miles I came to Watlington. This is a large village with a good range of amenities and one of those clock towers you can sit beneath at its centre. I popped into the shop and this time I satiated myself with biscuits and camembert.

I dived off of the B-road temporarily to pass through Lewknor, which resides in the shadow of the M40 and then I continued to Chinnor, which struck me as being unusual in having its facilities dotted about rather than concentrated in a single central area. There is a little railway here too, operating both steam and diesel hauled trains, but as it was slightly uphill to get to it, I just rode a 270-degree circuit of the place and then headed back to a pub called the Red Lion. It was 'beer o'clock.'

I headed to the quieter bar (the public bar if you like), where there was a screen showing a cricket match. This was being watched by a grandmother and two children who seemed far more interested in my maps and asking me where I'd been biking. The boy in particular seemed to have an affinity with cartographical sheets, and as we chatted a bit I realised why – his name was Adam.

"Can you guess what my name is?" I asked.

He got it in one!

Relishing all this attention, I decided to stay for a second pint. The grandmother was originally from Cork in Ireland. Adam pointed this out on the map, and also Ealing, where she lives now, as well as High Wycombe where they go to the cinema, and... you get the idea.

After this, I made my dash to Princes Risborough. The miles were falling away now. I serendipitously noticed a potential cycling route, as I came to a disused railway bridge. This was part of the Phoenix Trail, which runs from Princes Riz (as I shall henceforth refer to it) to Thame. I now had a reason to camp another night and elongate this trip for a third day, by riding to Thame, taking in Buckinghamshire's county town of Aylesbury and then riding the towpath of the Aylesbury Arm of the Grand Union Canal back to Tring. For now though, I followed another B-road back into 'The Riz' and asked a pedestrian where I could obtain that most healthy of foods, a kebab.

Soon I was in possession of a large doner, which was overflowing with salad. I heartily munched this nearby, with the sense of satisfaction that only a kebab can give. Powered up, I then headed off up a steep hill out of the town and took a left turn, right up into the wood at the top of the hill, ready for a possible reunion with The Ridgeway which would now be in 'footpath mode.'

Once things began to level out a bit, I dived into the forest and used my bike light to find a suitable spot to set up camp. From certain points in the woodland I could see the orange streetlights of the town below.

As I lay in the sleeping bag waiting for the zeds to come, I was a little startled to see a bright light seemingly coming in my direction. This happened several times, and puzzled me. I dismissed the idea that it was a car headlight shining into the wood from the lane, as the only sound I could hear was the hooting of an owl. I was well hidden though, so I fell asleep unperturbed. I had no idea of the torment that awaited.

****

The rain began at around 5am. I pulled the tarpaulin over myself and drifted back to sleep, but the pitter-patter was getting more persistent. By 9am it was obvious that there was to be no let up, and I routinely found myself pouring off rivulets of water that had settled on the tarp.

As I lay in relative warmth and comfort, my plan was to psyche up and then pack everything away in a mad dash, jump on the bike, freewheel back into the town and dive under that clock tower for cover while contemplating the next phase. This I did, and it all went well until I realised that I was 'sans phone.'

In the modern world 'sans phone' is a very uncomfortable place to be, so I hastily ripped everything back out of the rucksack and found my treasured smartphone zipped up inside the sleeping bag, which was now of course a bit 'Marti Pellow' - wet, wet, wet!

As I glided down the steep hill, jets of water streamed off of my wheels, making the compulsory shower feel more like a bath. The rain was coming down in stair-rods. I may as well have just bought a bottle of shampoo and killed two birds with one stone by washing my hair as I rode.

I spent a few minutes underneath the clock tower where a van driver was having a cigarette. I have never been a smoker, but I imagined that little bit of warmth emanating from the fag to be something profoundly comforting.

I then made my way to a café and ordered the only thing that would really do the trick on a day like today – a 'full English.' An elderly couple furnished me with some information about the town as I sat at a table in the far corner of the room. For me this was 'game over.' I was throwing in the towel (although that was exactly what I needed). I would have to return to ride the Phoenix Trail another time.

As I left, I decided to make use of the facilities in Tesco's again, but this time I felt no compulsion to buy anything. The rain had washed away my scruples as far as *that* was concerned. The railway station was about a mile through leafy suburbs to the south of the town. I reached it via what looked like a private road. Sadly, the capacity for a soaking grew even more when I took a wrong turning at the end and had to ask for yet more directions.

The train expedited me to Marylebone Station in Central London through hazy looking hills doused in precipitation. I was not looking forward to the saturation I was going to get cycling to St Pancras either. As ever, this was a adrenaline-pumping trek along London's inner ring road, pounding along intermittent bus lanes and wishing the taxi drivers wouldn't get so close. A wing mirror on my bike would come in very handy on busy roads like this. Actually, forget that, a car would be better!

During the following February I would return to the area on a day trip to complete the circuit I'd planned for my third day, beginning my ride wearing a woolly hat and tucking into a bacon roll at Princes Risborough station. The lane leading to the Phoenix Trail was flooded, but the rail trail itself was very pleasant, although riding it in the opposite direction would have provided nicer views, with the ridge of hills gradually getting closer.

Thame was a pleasant little town and Aylesbury was something of a clone town, but had a thriving market (the stall selling old coins interested me in particular). There was also a 'clock' consisting of a cylinder with numbers on the side that slowly fills with water. Presumably when it reaches the 'twelve' at the top, it all gushes out again. There was one for the days of the week too, but this was clearly incorrect as it was saying 'Friday' and I was definitely not at work.

Finding an outlet of a ubiquitous pub chain, a man stared intently at my pub lunch. Upon offering him a chip, it seemed that I had made a potential friend for life. The canal ride eastward from the town was less amicable - a partially flooded mud-bath. I eventually headed back onto the tarmac to ride back to Princes Risborough via Wendover – this time on the undulating B-road that bumps up and down the bottom part of the ridge. Dusk fell, my phone battery died and by then there was just one place I wanted to go – home.

NORTHAMPTONSHIRE & LEICESTERSHIRE (GRAND UNION CANAL)

10) Foxton's Flight

This next adventure was preceded by two day trips to check out the towpath of the Grand Union Canal between Central London and Leighton Buzzard. Both of these day trips began at Watford Junction station. Although inside the M25, Watford falls within Hertfordshire. The canal is accessed via parkland to the west of the town.

Heading north, it was a bendy, pleasant ride to begin with, but it began to feel more urban once outside the M25, where it is accompanied by the main railway line to Milton Keynes and the Midlands and passes through some yuppified sections in Hemel Hempstead and Berkhamstead.

I stopped for a beer at a pub beside the canal and continued via the deep Tring Cutting. Beyond this the canal begins to descend, curving furiously where the aforementioned Ayelsbury Arm departs, with the towpath reverting to grass until the approach to Leighton Buzzard, a small town where I eschewed the notion of camping in January in favour of a toastie in Costa and a train ride home.

The second day trip I did was heading south from Watford along the canal. The route via Rickmansworth was surprisingly rural in spite of being at the very edge of Greater London. Beyond this, the canal took a dead straight course, passing lakes. At the junction near Hayes, the canal's main line continues straight down to The Thames, while I decided to follow the branch that heads eastward towards Central London.

The canal passes through marshy parkland and later there is an aqueduct over the North Circular Road. I paused for a pint in a pub before pounding the final miles to Paddington, which is where the Regent's Canal takes over the route to link it with The Thames and the Lee Navigation at Limehouse.

That's enough about day trips. We're rewinding three months to June and it's time for me to explore the more northerly section of this mighty canal, linking London and the Midlands, so one muggy evening after work, I got the train up to Long Buckby in Northamptonshire.

"Why Long Buckby?" I hear you ask.

Well, this is the furthest you can get in a north-westerly direction with a Southeastern railcard. Yes, a railcard is a very useful thing to reduce the fares to a slightly less eye-watering level, but it is only valid for the region where you live, so it is best practice to purchase one ticket to the outer reaches of that region to get a third off the price and then buy any onward tickets separately.

In fear that we might be getting a bargain, there are even more caveats to having a railcard of this kind. For example, you can only use them off-peak and there's even a minimum fare on weekdays just so that you can't get any sort of deal for travelling to work. Punish the workers – always a good policy, hey?

It feels as though the rail companies are trying to trick us, so it is necessary to be one step ahead, like in some kind of Holmes and Moriarty scenario. For this you will need finely honed skills in research, logic, deduction and arithmetic. Oh yes, and it helps to have oodles of cash too.

As my train from Euston ventured out towards exotic Milton Keynes, I recall a gaggle of Friday night party girls raising the decibel level in the carriage to danger levels, so when I finally alighted at dusk at the bottom of Long Buckby village (in the middle of nowhere), I felt an immediate contrast.

The lane headed up a long hill to the centre, and the village had what I'd describe as a 'northern feel' to it, although really I wasn't that far north. I then descended the slope on a lane, heading northward through lush fields of green and gold, still vibrant in the hazy twilight. I was in serious need of a woodland, away from houses, but I soon realised that I wasn't going to get this, so I dived into a copse by the side of the road, which was the equivalent of burrowing through a hedge.

I found myself in another world, where the ground was covered in dark-green ivy. I initially threw my sleeping bag straight down on the deck, but I could feel the foliage through the bag as I tried to relax, so out came the tarp as a groundsheet.

This really wasn't a great spot to camp. Even the slightest incline means that during the course of the night both the tarpaulin and sleeping bag will move, and what's more, the ivy had some kind of sticky coating, so putting your arms out of the 'kip sack' was not advised. Thus, it took a long time to get to sleep and I could hear the steady breeze gradually increasing as the night went on.

****

70

To be honest, I couldn't wait to get out of that little copse. It was the worst campsite I'd chosen since Glastonbury and that was a long time ago (see the 'Somerset' section of this book). A bee was buzzing around me, which ensured that I was ready to hit the road at the unearthly hour of 6.45am. It was with a sense of relief that I pummelled my way through the foliage, back out to the road and fresh air.

I wended my way along the lane back to Long Buckby and then headed west to Watford, of Watford Gap fame. Yes, *that* Watford!

It was one of those 'blink and you miss it' places, and after riding right through the village, I backtracked to pick up the lane to the Leicester Line of the Grand Union Canal. Info from the Canal and River Trust website informs that the main line of the canal was built to improve communications from Birmingham and The Midlands to London (prior to this the only link to The Thames was via the Oxford Canal, completed in 1790). The Grand Junction Canal from Braunston Junction to The Thames was fully opened in 1805.

Other branches were added, and in 1894 the Grand Junction bought the canals which now comprise the Leicester Line, which joins the main line at Norton Junction, a couple of miles south from where I joined the waterway today near Watford. The Grand Union is an amalgamation of various canals and was not christened with this 'umbrella' name until 1929.

A path led down just before the bridge, and soon I was back in that blissful world of quaint, brick, humpback bridges over a meandering ribbon of water beneath arched trees. There were gentle hills to the left and right and it immediately felt like home; I can now see why narrowboating is such a popular pastime.

The towpath was not surfaced and involved riding over a lot of tree roots, but before very long at all I reached Crick Tunnel, so the path led steeply up to a lane for me to ride over the top.

I was looking for a byway or some kind of route back to the canal, but with signage non-existent, I eventually resorted to asking a male dog-walker for directions. He explained that the only way was via the village of Crick whilst one of his dogs tried to knock me off my bike. So I headed through the village, turned right and soon I was back in 'canal country.'

Then, just as I was settling into the habit of counting down the numbered bridges while admiring the pleasant scenery, the worst thing possible happened – I got a puncture. I had no puncture repair kit and vowed never to travel without one again.

I continued on shanks's pony, with the aim of walking to the nearest place that might possess a bike shop. As with most annoyances, this combined with a stored backlog of previous irritations in my mind to create a general ambience of life being pretty 'pants.' You could call it the 'compounding of misery' theorem if you wanted to sound like you know your stuff.

This was the first time I had undertaken one of these cycling missions since knowing my future wife (remember, the business card that went to Russia?). Until this trip she had no idea that I camped alone in unknown woodlands, so naturally concern about my safety had been expressed, along with attempts to persuade me not to go or to stay in a B&B instead. But I was unperturbed and wanted to demonstrate how safe and pleasant these trips could be, and now my mission had been cut short by a poxy thorn!

On top of that, my 'phone a friend' friend, whose daily messages were something of a link to home while out on these adventures, had suddenly gone into 'unresponsive' mode, so at this point I felt completely cut off and deflated (like my tyre). I fired off a message in frustration (all too easy with mobile technology) and continued my stomp along the canal bank.

One of my three camping buddies when faced with such a situation would probably ask himself, 'What would the Kings of Leon do?' and crack open a beer, but even if I knew the answer to that question, it would be about as much use as a chocolate fireguard.

After perhaps fifteen minutes of wandering beneath a metaphorical black cloud, I spotted a narrowboat. I was sorely in need of info, so I asked the man on board where the nearest bike shop was. He explained that it was probably in Market Harborough, a good ten miles away, but then he came up with a better idea – puncture repair. To top it all, he offered me a coffee while I repaired it. To paraphrase another one of those camping pals, 'How good is that?'

I pumped up the rubber inner tube and plunged it into the canal to identify where the puncture was from the bubbles, while my rescuer cut some squares out of the rubber strap on an old pair of goggles, for his puncture kit had everything I needed except rubber patches.

I then drank my coffee and he told me a bit about his lifestyle which seemed positively idyllic, living on the narrowboat and working in a nearby town. He was saying that the hedges along the canal had recently been attacked with a strimmer so the towpath wasn't recommended for cycling at all.

As I drained my cup, I could see that my tyre had stayed inflated for the duration, so it was time to get 'on the road again' and the song by Canned Heat came into my mind as I thanked him and wandered away.

How strange it is that when something positive happens, all of a sudden other positive things occur. You could call this 'the compounding of positive things' theorem if you wanted to sound like you know... ah - *deja vu!*

Thus, my 'phone a friend' friend decided to phone and apologised for his reticence to communicate. We had a good chat about my adventure and his recent dating experiences (remember the angsty call in Goring?) and after this I decided to tempt fate and ride a little section of the towpath, just as far as the next road bridge, which was numbered '45.'

This was the A4304 road to Market Harborough. I turned right and climbed the hill into the village of Husbands Bosworth, where I went into a post office for supplies and promptly found a pub for breakfast. Now I was living again!

Husbands Bosworth now reminds me of Overton from the 'Hampshire / Test Valley' section of this book, for it is similar in terms of size and its layout, with a waterway in a valley to the north and a crossroads at the centre. As I sat in a back bar, an old man chatted to me from his bar stool. The barmaid also advised me about the road to Market Harborough, the main thrust of my questioning being, 'Are there any hills?' I moved around to the main bar for a while before I left and the lunchtime tourists began drifting in.

The six miles to Market Harborough were OK, but I was fighting my asthma a bit. I found the town to be bustling for a small place and I read a plaque depicting various battles that had taken place in the area. If you'll excuse the coarseness, I couldn't help but paraphrase the popular mug motif; 'Same ****, different century!' I thought to myself.

I was still in search of a bike shop and was informed that there was nothing like that in the centre, although there was a branch of Halfords on the east side of the town.

I emerged from the shop, feeling much more comfortable with this towpath riding lark because I now had a puncture kit. So I returned to the town centre and climbed the hill, leaving on the northbound road and eventually picking up the Market Harborough Arm of the Grand Union Canal at a marina, which had the usual yuppyish feel that marinas have.

This four-mile branch canal meets the main thrust of the Grand Union's Leicester Line at Foxton. I was looking forward to this, as this is the location of a famous flight of locks, so great scenery was pretty much a 'given.' This branch began in a meandering style, heading south and then gradually rotating clockwise like the needle of a compass to north, and then back to west, by which time I was out of the leafy suburbs and enjoying glimpses of the countryside through the big hedge that bounded the canal.

However, tiredness was encroaching, and halfway along this section I finally capitulated. I laid down on the bank beside the towpath, and using my rucksack as a pillow, I had a little snooze. There is something uniquely pleasurable about an outdoor nap in the middle of the countryside. No work to return to, no obligations, no rules. Freedom.

I eventually roused myself and my legs felt rather stiff as I slowly got back into the flow of cycling. Two miles later I was at the narrowboater's paradise of Foxton.

I crossed the canal via a bridge and then wandered around what felt like a boating theme park. There was the impressive flight of locks to walk up, as well as the remains of the 'inclined plane' lift to view. This was designed to speed up the journey of boats between the lower and higher levels of the canal. Rather than use the time consuming method of waiting for a whole series of successive locks to fill or empty, you would merely float into a water filled 'bath' which was then hauled up the side of the hill ready for you to sail out at the top.

Ingenious though it was, this lift was only in use from 1900 to 1911, because soon after, the canals fell out of use. It would be many years before the tourist trade revitalised the life of these waterways, so all that remains of the lift is the grassy slope and a few grooves.

I had one of those moments where I needed to decide on the next part of my route. I'd learned that the section of the canal to Leicester was not surfaced, and to be honest I'd had enough of that kind of ramshackle biking for one day, but I wanted to see the city all the same. The only thing to do was to pop into a pub and mull it over with a pot of tea, washed down with a pint and a half of real ale.

A plan formed as the conversations entwined around me in the spacious dining area with its attached conservatory. I finally decided to do some 'sane biking' for a bit, so I headed up to the top of the flight of locks and rode along the undulating narrow lanes via the villages of Gumley and Saddington. Between the two was Saddington Reservoir, which served the function of a large fishing lake. The road then became wider, and when I reached the large village of Fleckney I popped into a Chinese take-away and was soon seated on a park bench, stuffing my face with chow mein and curry. This experience was only slightly marred by the gang of noisy teenagers sitting nearby.

I remember the streets leaving the village having rows of terraced housing and the place had the general feel of a small town. Later, there were some cattle grids and open, grassy verges between the lanes. Beyond was a long, slow descent towards the canal which was now taking an east-west course several miles to the south of Leicester. The air was cool and dusk was falling. I looked at various copses as I passed, assessing their suitability for camping, but before long I was back at the canal.

I turned left to follow the towpath westward, ultimately Leicester-bound. I rode a narrow strip of dirt through the grass. There were a few locks and the scenery was fairly open and pastoral, but places to get some kip were not forthcoming. I emerged onto an A-road at Kilby Bridge, but knew that beyond this the waterway would get more suburban - not conducive to surreptitious camping - so I backtracked, eventually finding a spot where I could hide behind the hedge which bounded the canal.

I positioned some branches around my sleeping bag to try to hide myself from early morning dog-walkers, but all in all, I felt that this spot was a million times better than last night's hole in the hedge. No walkers passed as I prepared for the 'sandman', but a few aircraft soared overhead, no doubt making their way to Leicester Airport.

11) Lesson in Leicester

Nobody spotted me as I lay in my sleeping bag behind the thicket in the hours between sunrise and when I decided to rise at 8am.

Sometimes, I wonder what it is that makes us rise at a particular moment. I don't mean when its a workday and the heart-attack-inducing beep of an alarm goes off about six inches from one's head, but I mean on a day like this, where there are no obligations or deadlines. It could almost provoke questions about destiny – is free choice just an illusion?

Stephen Hawkins depicted a theory of a four-dimensional universe in his book 'A Brief History of Time,' this being that the universe is basically a ball in four dimensions; three of space and one of time. It's hard to visualise, I know, but let's try, hey?

The Big Bang, when the universe is just a single point, is at the North Pole. It expands as we move towards the equator and then at the bottom as gravity becomes stronger than the force throwing all matter apart, it all falls back together into a single point at the South Pole.

Now, humans are basically just a collection of particles, like everything else, so if you view this four-dimensional globe like a map showing where every particle in the universe is at any given time, you realise that things cannot be any other way than the way they are. Freedom of choice becomes an illusion. Thus, we think we are making decisions every day, but basically we are just 'particle puppets.' Well, that's how I interpret the theory anyway. That's my thought for the day. From here on, it's downhill all the way.

When I reached the main road at Kilby Bridge again, I was desperate for the loo (see what I mean?), but the pub by the bridge was several hours from opening and there were no public toilets. I asked a man passing by where the nearest loo was and he replied something like 'On Saturn.' Well, actually he said 'In Leicester,' but it wouldn't have been any worse.

So on I pressed, trying to ignore my discomfort. The canal skirted some of the city's southern suburbs, with houses on the north side and countryside to the south. Then, the residences seemed to dwindle away for a while, until I reached an area where fishermen were setting up for a day's aimless yanking. It was Sunday after all.

Personally, I've never really seen the appeal of angling. I can understand fishing for food, but just hooking a fish out a body of water, looking at it and chucking it back seems about as daft as things can get. The 'relaxing in a chair drinking beer' bit I get, but I can't see what can be added by hoping a small, scaly thing gets a spike of metal stuck through its cheeks and finds itself whisked up into the air before being manhandled by a half-inebriated *homo sapien*. The other thing is, you have to keep lifting your bike over the rods.

After this leafy section, things opened out into one of those nature reserves that you often get on the edge of large towns – all marshy land and reeds, with a few walks criss-crossing through. The final mile into the city was wide, dead straight and creatively named 'The Mile Straight.'

I came off at a road bridge and headed east into the centre, which was about half a mile away. It was half ten in the morning and tiredness suddenly hit me like a brick wall. I decided to do the only sensible thing I could think of and head for McDonald's for a cup of tea and a *filet 'o' fish*.

Being English I usually pronounce this square of fish in a bun as 'fillet of fish,' but most staff repeat back 'one *fillay*' when reciting the order to correct me, yet 'fillay oh fish' doesn't really roll off the tongue, so this always makes me chuckle. It's been making me chuckle for twenty years at least.

I made a social phone call near a clock tower at the centre of the pedestrianised shopping area, and after this, I decided to explore.

I find exploring larger towns and cities something of a challenge, and when it comes to listing the UK's most populated places Leicester is pretty much 'up there.' With the smaller places I can usually encapsulate the feel of things within an hour or so of wanderings, but with larger places it seems like a gauntlet has been laid down to take in all the attractions in a similar timescale and still gain a comprehensive overview of the place. So where did I go first?

I walked to the railway station to assess the train fares.

I then wandered through an empty market square and out on the opposite trajectory to Abbey Park.

There was a miniature steam railway for children and I made my Skype call to Moscow on a park bench nearby. My girlfriend was now more relaxed, for she could see from the screen that I had not been gouged, savaged, ripped or ravaged in the wild and that I was actually having a very pleasant time.

The abbey ruins were more like foundations, but there was a cottage in the corner of these. I then found another bench by an open area of parkland and consumed the remainder of the chow mein, while people played ball games on the grass. I concluded my walk by picking up the canal (which runs much further north towards Nottingham) and heading back to the bridge where I had exited earlier that morning. By now, it was 'beer o'clock' and I headed for a large pub outlet where I quaffed a pint of mild and charged my phone in a wall socket, with permission of course.

It was at this point that I mused about these trips. For this had been my first trip away involving camping for almost two years. Today had been less of a hard core thrash and more of a leisurely exploration of a city – the kind of thing I often do with my girlfriend. I wondered if my life was changing and that eventually, I would phase out these solo trips and just do the city breaks in tandem.

In hindsight, I think this was merely a case of 'getting back into it,' for as you have already read, I have engaged in several more of these adventures since the Grand Union weekend. I think life is big enough for both kinds of touring.

It was time to visit the cathedral next, and it seemed to be one of the country's smaller ones. I was surprised to see Richard III portrayed in a good light. I had always imagined him to be particularly brutal, so I decided to visit the museum in order to find out more.

As every schoolboy knows, he was killed at the Battle of Bosworth Field in 1485, which saw off the House of York with the ascendency of the House of Tudor, but not a lot of people know that he had one thing in common with Kurt Cobain, apart from being dead, this being a back condition which makes one shoulder higher than the other.

'Dick the Bad' had also been in the news prior to my visit, due to an archaeological dig taking place at a car park at Greyfriars, where the king was believed to be buried. A skeleton was found and DNA tests later verified the similarity with the descendants of Richard III's sister.

There was an author there promoting a book on the subject, as well as a reasonably balanced portrayal of the king. Much of what we think about him comes from Shakespeare's play, which was of course aimed at a Tudor audience. An alternative viewpoint postulated that Richard III had a healthy level of empathy towards the poor and made laws protecting the common man.

Of course he is famed for being appointed to look after the two princes, the twelve-year-old King Edward V and his younger brother, by keeping them in the Tower of London. They disappeared soon after Richard himself took the throne, but again the murder of the boys is a matter of conjecture. Some folk even believe that the princes escaped.

I had a look around the medieval guildhall next – a splendid timber-framed hall that I can imagine once being used for decadent banquets. By now I felt that I'd 'done Leicester,' at least in a rudimentary sense, and I made my way to the station, this time with my bike, ready to move on. My next port of call was Rugby, but for some reason I asked for a single to Derby and ended up returning to the window with a slightly clearer head.

I had to change trains at Nuneaton, and as there was quite a substantial wait I decided to head for the nearest pub. There was a typical Sunday afternoon crowd inside (mostly male), and a jazzy version of Rage Against The Machine's 'Killing in the name of' was emanating from the speakers. I was duly impressed, in the same way as when I first heard Radiohead's 'Just' given the Mark Ronson/Phantom Planet treatment. What a cultured day I was now having.

And so to Rugby.

There are not many towns with a sport named after them, so I expected high things. The legend has is that in 1823 William Webb Ellis decided to stick two fingers up to the rules of football and picked up the ball and ran with it at Rugby School. This is probably something of a myth, although the international committee did name the Rugby world cup 'The William Webb Ellis Trophy.'

The town centre was fairly unremarkable and after a brief wander I settled on a Lloyd's Number One bar for some food. These are a kind of 'Wetherspoons' with a couple of quid bunged on the prices. Anyway, I had a nice curry and then I ventured out of the town due south-east, using lanes, passing green playing fields, beneath a cloudless blue sky.

As I continued, I encountered a few undulations and bridged the M45 (surely one of the quietest motorways in the UK) as well as the Oxford Canal. I was heading for a village called Barby. At the time I was trying to push an irritating song out of my head: "I'm a Barby girl, in a Barby world..."

There was a steep climb before I got to this village and a long panoramic descent to cross the A361 – an epic of a road that runs from Ilfracombe in Devon to Kilsby, about three miles to the north of this point.

Soon I was back at the Grand Union Canal, this time the main thrust of the canal that runs from Birmingham (which allegedly has more miles of waterway than Venice) via Royal

Leamington Spa and on to London. I joined it just to the east of Braunston Tunnel, which is just to the east of Braunton Junction – a significant location in the canal world, appearing on mileage posts all the way along the canal to London.

It was nice to be back on the towpath, although it was just grass again. This section seems popular with narrowboats and soon I reached Norton Junction where the Leicester Line branches off. There was a very pleasant pub just beyond this point and I ordered a refreshing glass of tonic water from a friendly, young barmaid who seemed genuinely interested in my adventure. I sat outside on a bench enjoying the boating vibes and then continued my ride on the other side of the A5 bridge.

I braced myself for a noisy section of the towpath, running between the M1 and the railway line. With the locks all inclined downward, this seemed fitting as my route was now heading south, down the country. It's funny how it always seems to be uphill going north and downhill heading south.

I mused on how four eras of transport conduits were now running side by side. First you had the A5, which was part of the Roman road, Watling Street, running from Dover, via London, to Wroxeter in Shropshire. Then there was the Grand Union Canal of course, then the railway line and finally the mighty M1 – the UK's second longest motorway (the M6 takes the crown).

The motorway eventually branched away from the other three, like a young upstart determined to do things its own way, and the canal became remarkably pleasant as it wound its way around a number of villages. It seemed to meander at a level slightly above the valley carved out by the River Nene, and around Nether Heyford I decided to branch off and start thinking about a campsite.

I rode through the village, which seemed very pleasant and then took a lane northward towards the river, with views of the significant hillside beyond the motorway. Serendipitously, I spotted a little byway heading east. As it rounded a right angle bend, there was a deep enough copse running beside the trail for me to deviate off and find a little grotto in the trees. With just a field to one side and a sparsely used byway hidden from view on the other, this was the best camping spot I'd found on this three-day mission.

A nightingale sang as it grew dusky, and although the ground seemed to retain the cold and my asthma gave me a little bit of grief, I was glad that I'd opted to camp a third night, which would enable me to continue along the canal and check out Northampton and Milton Keynes, hopefully bringing me to Leighton Buzzard, a point beyond which I had already ridden the Grand Union further south. This was my plan at least.

12) Milton Keynes Meltdown

The M1 created a steady roar throughout the night, but it was more a soporific drone than a deafening irritation. I was ready for action at 7am and was soon packed up and heading back to the village of Nether Heyford.

Now, in normal everyday life, if I get the chance, I will not rise until at least 9am, yet it struck me that in natural surroundings it is much easier to get up early. Having researched this, it seems that before the invention of the electric light, people would go to sleep soon after sunset and usually rise with the dawn. As a result, folk had longer nights of sleep and the body naturally ensured a waking hour in the middle. David K Randall points out in his book Dreamland that old literature often refers to 'first sleep' and 'second sleep,' which was clearly the norm at the time.

Personally I think it is a much healthier way to live. It seems that most of us 21st century schizoid men (a King Crimson reference there just to keep the 'musos' awake) have been victims of anxiety, depressive thoughts, etc. at some point or another, and it would seem that a good night's sleep, simple though it sounds, is the most effective measure at avoiding such problems. If dreams are the brain's filing system, it seems logical to deduce that without sufficient opportunity to dream, the filing system becomes chaotic and irrational thought patterns result. Modern life is literally making us mad!

Modern life seemed to have intruded little upon Nether Heyford, for it was in possession of both a butcher's shop and a bakery. I went up a little path along the edge of a field to rejoin the canal and continue my south-eastward pedal. The scenery was something of an anticlimax though, presenting me with long, grassy straights to ride and none of the meandering scenery I had become used to. This was proper farming country.

The next junction was with the spur of the canal to Northampton, but I decided to continue on a little and use the road instead, purely for speed. I rode along a lane that ran beside the Northampton Arm and then bridged it, heading across a little valley to the village of Milton Malsor.

I turned left onto what appeared to be one of the original main roads into Northampton, now superseded by a dual carriageway. This took me up a long, suburban hill with the odd roundabout thrown in for good measure. It was a fairly uninteresting drag to be brutally honest. From the top, it was a long, straight descent into Northampton, eventually bridging the canal and River Nene to reach the centre.

I chained up my bike near the central market square and set out to explore. It was not long after 9am, and it amazed me to have done so much before the time I would usually be thinking about getting out of bed.

After a wander, I popped into a café where you could create your own breakfast from a list of ingredients. I got chatting to the man at the till and asked him, "What are the tourist attractions in Northampton?"

The reply wasn't so inspiring; "Basically, there aren't any!"

But he did inform me that it claims to be the largest town in the UK that hasn't been given city status. As with all such superlatives I filed this info in my mind to fact-check at a later date. I saw on the map that the town does have a cathedral, conclusive proof that this does not necessarily give a place city status.. However, being located around a mile to the north of the centre, I lost heart as I began biking through the suburbs towards it and did a U-turn.

I believe this was the first time I'd encountered one of those superstores that sell used CDs and DVDs for prices as low as £1, giving the online retailers a run for their money.

The issue of the questionable tax practices of some of these Internet giants is a thorny subject for me. With most High Street book chains only interested in big publishers and blockbusters, the net seems to be the only viable outlet for independent authors to get their work 'out there.' But I disagree strongly with the way certain unavoidable websites (as well as some High Street chains) use loopholes to avoid tax. We want an NHS, a fair welfare system, independent education, transport that doesn't cost the earth, etc. so we need these big boys to pay their fair share just as we have to.

Sometimes the argument is put forth that, 'If we didn't avoid the tax, we wouldn't be able to provide the jobs,' but if 'anything goes' to create jobs, we may as well start filling our fields with opium poppies or flogging weapons to brutal dictators. Actually, hang about, we already do the second one, don't we?

Back to my ride before I get accused of 'carping on:'

I had some trouble locating a road to get me down to the canal which I intended to ride back to the Grand Union, but eventually I found myself pedalling along its south bank, passing beneath modern bridges and leaving urbanity behind. I was surprised by the flight of locks leading upward which could have almost rivalled Foxton, although these were a bit more spaced out. After about six miles I reached the junction again and continued my southward jaunt along the main line of the Grand Union.

It wasn't long before the canal plunged into Blisworth Tunnel. It is very rare for the towpath to accompany the canal through the tunnel, so this meant a climb up to the roadside. In the days of horse-drawn barges, this would have necessitated taking the horses up over the hillside and using self-propulsion on the subterranean route. This often meant laying flat and walking along the tunnel wall with one's feet.

I remember the scenery along the lane route being very open at the top of the hill, and as I descended I noticed a path on my left leading back down to the canal. A short way beyond this I came to the village of Stoke Bruerne which was positively idyllic. If you imagine the canal as the village's High Street with pubs and other outlets along the towpath on either side, this was Stoke Bruerne in a nutshell.

There was a downward lock at the southern end near the road bridge, as well as a museum on all things canal related. The pub seemed to call louder to me than any other amenity.

I popped in and ordered a local brew, pausing to admire the old fashioned skittle area. The wooden interior of the pub gave me a relaxed, mellow feeling, and upon draining my glass I took a few photos while a lock-keeper helped some narrowboaters to close the gates and drain out the water, thus descending to the next level.

The section of canal beyond the bridge was less inspiring to be honest. The scenery seemed to flatten out and I was back on a grass surface, which is quite frankly hard work on a bike. I passed a narrowboat being piloted by a group of young people in their late teens or early twenties, only for them to regain their lead when I felt in serious need of a rest and decided to lay on a bank for a while, listening to the happy voices in the beer garden of the pub on the opposite side of the water.

I stoically continued, and passed the young boat enthusiasts a third time as I rode. Things became more interesting as I passed over the 101-foot-long Cosgrove Aqueduct which carried the canal over the River Great Ouse. It was built in 1811 to replace an earlier brick structure. As I admired the view of the pastures below, I was re-energised. I was now heading for Milton Keynes and I imagined a bustling riverside scene of trendy bars and marinas awaiting me. Hey, I might even get one of those Trappist Belgian beers somewhere.

My spirits remained optimistic as the canal turned eastward around Wolverton and New Bradwell, and as it turned to head south again near the edge of Newport Pagnell, I found that the towpath had become too narrow to safely ride, so I went onto the parallel roadway.

This continued with poplar trees, all equidistant, lining the route as it curved, first one way, then the other. It went on, and on, and on. Where were the yuppie watering holes I had imagined? Where was the metropolitan waterside scene a la Bristol? No, it was just 'tree, tree, tree, curve, tree, tree, tree, curve, tree, tree...' Well, you the idea – I felt that I was getting nowhere, trapped in a never-ending vortex, without even the slightest variation in scenery to give a sense of progression

Maybe this is what heaven could be like after a while. It was all very pleasant and green, but now I longed for an ugly great monstrosity of a factory belching smoke into the air, or a huge great Tesco mega-giga-superstore to break the monotony, or even an industrial sized Travelodge poking a concrete finger into the sky. I can't believe I am writing this, but I think what you are witnessing is something called 'The Milton Keynes Effect.' Everything is so controlled and uniform that one hankers for some chaos after a while.

As a writer of short stories, I could envisage an A.I./Matrix-esque plot set in the future, where intelligent life makes contact with the earth, long after the era of humans has passed. They would be able to use the traces of human DNA to resurrect the consciousness of individual people in a virtual reality world made out of their favourite memories (assuming an advanced civilisation would be kindly, that is).

Each person could then live in their own personal heaven, but after a while, one by one, they might get bored with nice things and no challenges. They might even wish for some hardship to give some kind of meaning to the relentless pleasures. The alien race would then grant this wish and would tweak the virtual worlds of the humans time and time again, and eventually you would end up with life as we know it. Although I think they might choose to leave some of the more horrific facets of humanity out like war, violence and the music of Justin Bieber. Maybe I had discovered the purpose of Milton Keynes – a dream of heaven designed by an alien race of town planners.

All I could see was that I wasn't going to get my Trappist Belgian beer, or artisan foodstuffs served with a pretentious sounding name. I was just going to get trees and curves, all identical, for mile after mile. And to make matters worse, there wasn't a soul around to ask for directions to civilisation.

Eventually, a teenage boy crossed my path and I asked him which way I should go to find the nearest shop or pub. In spite of being a lifelong resident of 'MK,' as he called it, this young lad was struggling to direct me to the nearest watering hole.

This was probably because Milton Keynes is laid out in a grid system. In most European towns and cities all roads ultimately lead to the centre. You only need to know which side of you the centre is on and you can easily negotiate a route and be sitting, relaxed with a cup of tea, in no time, but with a grid system, only one road in each direction is going to lead you to the heart of the conurbation; the rest will just bypass it, and before you know it you'll be surrounded by suburbs again.

I eventually made some sense of the youngster's instructions and found the pub. It was closed.

It looked like one of those box-shaped buildings thrown up in the 1960s, with, as a friend sometimes puts it, 'all the atmosphere of a municipal lavatory.' There was the obligatory 'small outlet of a big superstore' nearby too, so I popped in and asked for directions there.

I followed their instructions, and as I climbed a sterile, suburban hill, I heard a hiss, and before I knew it my tyres were flat. I could imagine my friend chanting, 'What would the Kings of Leon do? What would the Kings of Leon do?' as a pacifying mantra.

Relegated to shank's pony, I pushed my bike into the 'concrete and glass' town centre. People were bustling around the large shops, all located back from the road, USA-style, to allow for parking. Drained of energy, I just wanted to get to the railway station. As I walked, I witnessed a teenage boy pleading for his life in a subway.

"It's me! You know me!" he begged his thuggish assailant, who was clearly in such a haze of pure rage that he showed no mellowing of his aggressive stance. It was another one of those 'What should I do?' moments – should I call the police? Or is this normal here?

Everybody else was just walking past as though this behaviour was pretty standard stuff, reminding me of the futuristic people in the 1960s film version of HG Wells' 'The Time Machine,' casually picnicking by the riverbank while somebody drowns. In the end I did what any sane person would do and gave them both a 'What on earth are you doing?' look and continued walking.

As I reached the station, I was ready to conclude my visit to Milton Keynes. Sadly I didn't make it all the way to Leighton Buzzard, as was the original aim and no doubt I'll incorporate this missing link in my exploration of the Grand Union some time in the future when I feel ready to face Milton Keynes again.

Without wishing to be unbalanced, I can still see why people like MK. I imagine that the layout means that it doesn't have the congestion or parking problems of other towns which, let's face it, were designed for the horse and cart. It has ample shops and big names, and I'm sure the parks are very pleasant if one isn't looking for a nice glass of Chimay or Westmalle beer and a pot of olives served with a charcuterie board of cold meats. I had both of these options when I got to St Pancras. The two glasses on Chimay and the little pot of olives went down like... a snake's foot of course!

So, as I prepare to board the bullet train back to deepest, darkest Kent, we step into our 'Back to the Future' style DeLorean time machine and rewind further to an entirely different epoch within 'The Life of Adam' – a bit like the character in that story by HG Wells.

SOUTH DOWNS (WEST)

13) 'Cocking' it up!

21 months are now whizzing past us, as our time machine prepares to deposit us on a warm September day. I was still a single man at this time, but if you think this means that this book is about to take a turn into wild hedonism, I'm afraid I'm going to have to disappoint.

At the time of this particular trip, the life-changing business card was already in Moscow, but the recipient was merely an email buddy. As her visits to England became more frequent, my cycling trips became mere day trips for a while, and therefore aren't included in this book which is about actual adventures. And in 'Adam's Concise English Dictionary' an adventure is only an adventure if it includes camping. However, where these daytrips appear to complete a route documented in this book, I am giving a brief summary.

So, as we are about to turn our attention to the western half of the South Downs Way, I'll quickly tell you about two jaunts of mine that covered the eastern end.

22 months prior to this I'd ridden up to the South Downs Way from Falmer station, which is where you alight if you want to go to the University of Sussex or to watch a home game of Brighton and Hove Albion Football Club. It was a gruelling climb out of the suburbs along the lane to Ditchling Beacon, which is the highest point in East Sussex, in fact, any Sussex, at 814 feet above sea level.

I headed west, with stunning views from the top of the ridge. The route collapsed into the valley at Pyecombe where I had a 'soup stop' in a pub and crossed the A23. After more undulations on the trail, I got caught in a hailstorm at the top of the hills and dived straight into a pub at Bramber to dry off. I was duly impressed by the friendliness of the locals and decided to stay in a very affordable room at a pub in nearby Upper Beeding, from where I made a night-time amble up to the ruined castle. I cycled back eastward to Lewes on lanes for the train home the next day.

The county town of East Sussex was awash with activity, preparing for the Guy Fawkes celebrations that evening. I'm not sure what it is about the small Sussex towns and pyromania, but Rye also does a pretty mean fireworks display, but for burning effigies (the true rebellious spirit of the occasion, surely?) and fire filled trugs being wheeled through the streets, I think it has to be Lewes.

I would later return to Ditchling Beacon, to cover the trail to its eastern terminus at Eastbourne. However, I messed my route up and ended up in Lewes again, this time taking a look a look at Anne of Cleves' house (one of only two wives that outlived Henry VIII, keeping their heads while all around were losing theirs, so to say). I picked up the trail again at Southease. Cue another gruelling climb, before the nosedive into the picturesque village of Alfriston, where the route splits into two. I took the northern route continuing along the hilltop to Eastbourne (the southern route is the Seven Sisters / Beachy Head trail beside the English Channel).

So here we are, about to pummel the South Downs Way westward from Cocking. I caught my train to Chichester, and immediately headed out of the West Sussex cathedral city, westward past the college to pick up the Centurion Way which uses the trackbed of the old Midhurst railway line, curving away northward.

You may recall that this is the path where I would later lose my bike to a petty thief, so beware that [insert the plural of any four-letter-word of your choice here] operate in this area.

The area was busy with schoolchildren and I remember wandering about on a bank while I made a phone call to a friend with whom I used to exchange news of the latest gaffes made by our beloved politicians and those psychopathic business folk who would like a return to the Victorian 'send the boys up the chimneys' lifestyle for the proles.

As the former rail route continues, it passes by some earthworks. These are situated in a wide, grassy area and include an amphitheatre sculpture. My curiosity must have been at a low point as I didn't stop to check out this area more thoroughly.

At the village of Lavant, our route briefly takes us onto residential roads, but before long, the trackbed continues across the fairly flat countryside. However, this is short lived, as after another mile or so, it does a ninety-degree bend to the left at 'bike thief corner' and abandons the rail route completely.

I recall my disappointment when I travelled all the way to Chichester some years before to check out this route, to discover that it could only muster about four miles in length before changing course and climbing to meet the busy A286.

The next village is West Dean, where there is a 'lane' alternative for the briefest of times before one has to face the traffic on the A-road again until reaching Singleton. This is the point at which the road rounds a sharp bend, as if to admit that it had been avoiding the inevitable climb onto the hills before suddenly making a decision to 'go for it.'

Singleton is very pleasant, and I seem to recall the odd thatched cottage there. I am not sure if I managed to stoically steer myself away from the pub, or if it was merely closed at this quiet time of day (late afternoon), but I found my way to a tearoom and ordered myself a pot of tea and a treacle tart instead.

Then I faced the climb on the A286, which actually wasn't that bad. The scenery was more wooded now. Upon reaching the South Downs Way just before the village of Cocking, I turned left and began to follow this undulating route, which began with a deceptively hefty climb. As I neared the top of this, my 'phone and friend' friend phoned to talk about geocaches.

This hobby involves locating each 'cache' from a grid reference and signing a slip of paper to say you have discovered it. Nerdy as it may sound, it is a very popular worldwide activity. The caches are usually small, plastic containers hidden under benches, beneath rocks, within the roots of a tree, etc. although some bigger caches can take the form of a plastic lunchbox containing a selection of business cards from local authors trying to drum up a bit of trade. Well, actually, there are lots of other things in them too.

After this little chat, I continued, unconvinced to start searching for these little pots along my route. The path dived into a wood near Treyford Hill and promptly descended.

Now, when you're on the South Downs Way a descent is not a good thing, because what goes down always has to come back up again. The thing with this descent was that it was going on for far too long. The wide, grassy track through woodland eventually came out onto the B2141 road. With this being the pre-smartphone era (for me at least) I had just a few torn-out pages from a road atlas to navigate by. Glancing at these crumpled sheets, I deduced that I had lost 'The Way' and that I was a lot further south than I wanted to be. So I followed the road northward, and before I knew it, I had climbed all the way back up onto the ridge again, in the vicinity of Tower Hill.

As the road began to descend, I picked up the path which sheared off to the left, through more trees to an adjoining B-road. I was back on course. There were more ups and downs to be savoured and the route made use of a lane for a while just after passing into the county of Hampshire. When I reached another lane above the village of Buriton, I decided to take a right turn to descend and check out the village, which is located a few miles south of Petersfield.

I rode up the main street and back again, eventually resigning myself to waiting outside the pub on a bench for around fifteen minutes, as it was not yet evening opening time. How quaint!

Once inside, I perused some of the well-produced local history books and pondered what the production cost of such tomes might be while a large party of visitors from Devon ordered their drinks. And no, they weren't all drinking cider. We'll have no stereotypes here. An oldish man from the group chatted to me, while I made up my mind to order some salmon on a bed of spinach.

For a small village I was impressed to find two pubs, so after food, I thought I'd complete the pair. The second establishment showed promise, with classical music emanating from what I remember as a white, plastered passageway at the back. Maybe this was pumped in to chill the chefs out in the nearby kitchen. Chefs are a fiery bunch as we know from Gordon Ramsay and chums.

I ordered my drink and sat in a back-bar, but my opening gambit failed to engage the barmaid who appeared to be in her late teens and unable to respond to conversational stimuli, instead choosing the purely functional role of being the instrument for getting the beer from the pumps to the drinkers and relieving them of their cash.

I think we all know why landlords tend to choose young females as bar staff (although few would admit the obvious), but when you're a stranger in an unfamiliar place it is that little bit of conversation, from anybody, that tends to keep you there for a second drink.

The more seasoned bar steward knows this and knows exactly when to chat – just as you're entering that final third of the pint. However, I have often noticed that upon ordering another drink you are left alone to stare at the walls again while the member of staff returns to talk sweet nothings with the locals. They don't need it - they have each other to talk to - look after the stranger!

So, to avoid the prospect of working your way through a whole pint while trying to find meaning within the patterns on the seventies style wallpaper, I tentatively order a 'half' in these situations. This often throws the member of staff and it is thus possible to gain a whole fifteen minutes of extra conversation. Well, this was a remarkably short game of 'conversation chess,' so I necked my drink and decided to head back up into the hills.

When I got back to the point where the South Downs Way crosses, I turned right to get a nanometre or two further along my intended route, before finding a copse to dive into, just to the north of the trail. This seemed the perfect spot to camp.

And so, with groundsheet and sleeping bag laid out, I lay staring up at the moon, enjoying the tranquillity that comes before sleep and feeling thankful that my own company was slightly better than that of the barmaid.

14) Worshipful Winchester

I got up just after 9am. I *must* have been tired to sleep so late in the great outdoors. It always feel good to get back on the bike once everything is safely crammed back into my rucksack in the mornings. It's almost as though the camping and the biking form a kind of 'yin and yang' and that when you've had enough of one, the other is the perfect tonic.

I remember the South Downs Way descending into a country park, where I was taken onto tarmacked driveways before passing beneath the A3 and turning northward to run parallel with it.

I passed through an area which was being set up for some kind of public event. There were a few roadways which served as a parking area and I wondered if I had chosen the right route as signage was now more random.

Soon I knew I was on the right track from the way the grassy trail streaked straight up towards Butser Hill. As the incline was almost as vertical as price rises before Christmas, I was relegated to shanks's pony again, and even this felt like a rude awakening into the new day.

When I got to the top I was hot and the route came out onto a lane which was fairly flat and pastoral as it ran along the plateau. The path seemed to run parallel to the road behind a hedge / fence at times, but for me it was easier just to stay on the tarmac. Eventually I found a café in some kind of open garden / park. I wandered in and ordered myself a stilton and salad sandwich augmented with a pot of tea.

Beyond this I must have descended somehow, as I remember ominously approaching a steep hillside where the path suddenly turned sharply to the right to present me with the inevitable long, slow, diagonal climb through a strip of shrubby bushes. This brought me up to a lane where I turned left to pass a picnic site with a viewpoint back across the lower ground. 'The Way' then diverts off to the right to pass Old Winchester Hill, the site of an Iron Age hill-fort.

These 'ages' are often bandied about, but in a nutshell there are three and the names of the ages are taken from the predominant materials used to make tools. The oldest age, the Stone Age, is subdivided into three periods - Palaeolithic, Mesolithic and Neolithic.

The Palaeolithic era is so vast that it has three subdivisions of its own – lower, middle and upper. The era began around

700,000 years ago and ended when the last ice age ended at around 10,000BC with the dawn of the Mesolithic era.

Monuments that we will visit later in this book such as Avebury and Stonehenge are from the Neolithic era, which began at around 4,000BC when people abandoned hunter gathering and took up agriculture as a way of life. This period also marked the appearance of communal graves or 'barrows.' Just in case you have a rosy view of such times, average life expectancy was 35 for men and 30 for women.

At around 2500BC we come into in the UK Bronze Age, and then the Iron Age from 800BC until the Roman invasion in 43AD. At this point pre-history is taken to have ended as written records began.

To bring things right up to date, we then had the dark ages, the Renaissance, the industrial revolution, and we may be currently just nudging our noses into a possible new era – the information age. The fact that almost any info can be located at the merest touch of a few keys gives humans an intellectual power never known before. So are we at the dawn of a new era of objectivity, leading to greater understanding and peace?

Apparently not, as generally humans will tend to seek out information that confirms their already fixed views (like buying your favourite newspaper). Essentially the basic nature of our brains hasn't had sufficient time to evolve with the times, such changes requiring tens of thousands of years. The problem is that we are now monkeys in charge of nuclear weapons.

Anyway, there were a few 'apes in jackets' exploring the site on this September morning, and for the record, in spite of its name, the original capital of England and county town of Hampshire is still around a dozen miles away from this hill bearing its name.

I remember the path zigzagging around the edges of fields as it descended into the Meon Valley, with my thoughts being of the 'What on earth is it doing going over there?' variety.

Soon I'd reached the trackbed of the former Meon Valley railway. We will come to that later in this book, when we are nearing the 'Big Bang' that spewed forth this universe of cycling exploits. I briefly multiplexed with this gravel trail before diverting off to the village of Exton. Here I chatted to two ladies on horseback and then dived into a pub. There were maps on the wall (always the sign of a good alehouse) and I remember sitting in a side-room and watching a seemingly aristocratic guy and an American saying grace before eating their meal.

Biking is always an optimistic pastime, and after coming down a steep hill I always manage to convince myself that somehow the route is going to skirt around the hills and not present me with a reciprocal climb back up. This is nearly always wrong, and I remember the lane beyond Exton just going up and up and up, as it boldly dares to scale Beacon Hill. However, once one is at the top of this south-east-facing slope, the feel of the remainder of the long distance path is very different, for the route now follows a series of lanes and farm tracks which are generally pretty flat, and one at last gets the feeling of some serious progression towards Winchester. Ultimately, the ridge is less defined at this western end of the trail.

'The Way' then crosses the A272 road, a classic east-west route that was once part of an alternative to the Pilgrims' Way between Winchester and Canterbury. The only evidence of this is a solitary road sign at Newick in East Sussex, showing the distance to Winchester as 68 miles and Canterbury 63.

'The Way' then follows a 'permissive path' northward across farmland. I remember seeing rows of vines, among other crops and getting a sense of openness at this point. The route then turns left onto an undulating track, before heading left again and climbing back towards the A272.

At this point the heat seemed searing. My phone rang and this gave me an excuse to stop and rest on the bank by the path as I listened to the latest exploits concerning some nuisance neighbours. I was profoundly glad to be in deepest Hampshire, rather than on the receiving end of threats and loud music. And let's face it, whenever somebody plays music in an intrusive way, it's never anything good. Can you imagine banging on the walls shouting, 'Can you turn that music up please? The next track is the best one on the album!'

Once I'd crossed the A272 again, the path prepared for its final descent to Winchester (this sounds like an announcement on a passenger jet). I remember emerging onto some narrow lanes, but I couldn't find a route across the M3 and into the city, so I ended up on the A31, and merely turned left to bridge the motorway and descended to the centre with the flow of traffic.

I headed for the usual 'no alarms and no surprises' pub outlet and discovered that you got a free cup of tea with gammon, egg and chips, so I ordered that, and just in case you think I'm being a 'wuss,' I ordered a pint as well, so there! I then received another phone call but I struggled to hear anything in the busy bar-room. After this, I decided to explore.

I looked at the cathedral, which has the longest nave as well as the longest overall length of any Gothic cathedral in Europe. The New Vaudeville Band's sixties pastiche 'Winchester Cathedral' would have no doubt popped into my mind at this point. I know my mind well enough to be sure of this, even though I didn't make any notes about such detailed thought processes.

I then wandered around the quiet quarters of the city and ended up by the River Itchen. I sat by the gently flowing waters for some time, just watching the ducks and enjoying the tranquillity. Such moments are good for the brain, and I think perhaps this is why I like these rides so much.

These days if you visit your doctor with anxiety, depression or similar worries, you will more than likely be prescribed something called 'mindfulness.' Unlike Prozac or tranquillisers, it doesn't come in a cardboard box and it doesn't cost you any money. The discipline is little more than merely observing and enjoying one's own existence for a few moments, ignoring the white noise of frenzied activity. Personally, I think that the soothing sound of running water and the quack of a few ducks as warm sunshine beams down is far nicer than just sitting at home doing breathing exercises.

People often say that smoking relaxes them, but as far as I'm aware, the nicotine in cigarettes actually increases the heart rate, so I wonder if they are referring to the fact that it forces them to stop rushing around like headless chickens and concentrate on a bit of breathing. Obviously if the breaths contain carcinogens this isn't medically recommended, but once again if it gives them time to stop and stare, I can see their logic.

Like the TV news, I think modern life should come with a government health warning. It seems as though it is sadistically designed to make such relaxing moments impossible. As Pink Floyd sang on their monumental Dark Side of the Moon album, "Dig that hole, forget the sun / And when at last the work is done / Don't sit down, it's time to dig another one!"

The Welsh poet W H Davies was singing from the same hymn-sheet around 60 years earlier when he wrote, "What is this life, if full of care, We have no time to stand and stare?" I would add that as far as I can see, life is just a collection of experiences, so to me the obvious purpose would be to make these experiences as pleasant and varied as possible (while the necessity of work aims to do just the opposite). The most important thing to me seems to be able to turn around at the end of it all with a feeling of having lived, whatever that means individually.

Camping trips such as these have seemed instrumental in leading the way to happier days. In my case, this was from the ruins of an imploded pub rock band to meeting my future wife, but of course the thrust of this book is a backward journey, so this particular phoenix will be diving back into the ashes sometime near the end. Anyway, I'm not going to break into song at this point – this is a book, not a musical - but the basic lesson is to stop watching the bucks and start watching the ducks.

So when the time was right, I rose from my bench, and returned to main street. I began heading west on the steadily climbing Roman road that changes chameleon-like from pedestrianised High Street to B-road and then into the single-file Sarum Road, but it may as well have been called Memory Lane, for I was merely retracing part of the route I'd taken from Kent to Somerset during that epic hike in 2006. So in the interest of continuity, I already knew exactly where I was going to camp for the night. I crossed a north-south lane at a rural crossroads, and beyond this the woodlands encroached from the right. Then just as on that night in 2006, I dived into the trees and set up my bed for the night. The only difference was that this time I was alone; my former accomplice was no doubt in a cosy living room, maybe enjoying a glass of wine with his wife.

As dusk fell I decided to take a wander. This could be viewed as a test of suitability of the campsite, for if it is safe to leave my rucksack and sleeping bag (but nothing more valuable) unguarded for perhaps a quarter of an hour and return to find both untouched, then I can pretty much be sure that I won't be disturbed by axe-wielding maniacs at four in the morning. Of course if I returned to discover that either had disappeared, that would seriously put the mockers on things, but these little crepuscular ambles give one a sense of truly being at home in the woodlands and confident in one's surroundings.

A creature was making a noise that was a cross between a whistle and a howl at 1am, and as is so often the case, a wind blew up as the night progressed.

15) Southampton Sprint

The first sound I heard in the early morning was that of bicycle wheels whizzing along a nearby path. I was closer to civilisation than the dusky conditions when I set up camp had led me to believe

Clouds had gathered and I had soon stuffed everything back into my rucksack. As ever, the sleeping bag took up about 90% of the capacity. I had never quite mastered the art of compacting it into the little black bag that it came with, viewing this as a task akin to getting the squeezed-out contents of a tube of toothpaste back inside, complete with stripes intact. That said, I was often glad of having such a bulky sleeping bag, as it is one of those sacks you can apparently fling down on an Arctic ice sheet and still be cosy.

I returned to the crossroads along the Roman road and turned right to head southward, coming out onto an A-road to pass through the village of Hursley.

Once back into open countryside I thought I'd branched off onto the B-road to Chandler's Ford, but I ended up in a place called Otterbourne. The terrain had been pretty flat and consisted of fairly unremarkable farmland - a light yellowy green on your DIY store paint-chart, if you want to visualise it. Please note, nobody is paying me for product placement in this book, any retail outlets mentioned are merely there for factual continuity.

When product placement was first introduced on British TV the brand inclusions stuck out like a sore thumb. I even remember hearing the unwieldy phrase 'Life is like a packet of Revels' in one programme I watched. Anybody viewing the signals from outer space would believe that phrases such as 'You've had your Weetabix today' had suddenly become ingrained in British everyday conversation.

Since those early days, either the practice has been dropped or the insertions are becoming more subtle. Personally I think there are already enough ways for advertisers to assault our minds without filling up TV programmes with inane references to commercial products.

Anyway, by now the rain had begun and I dived into a bus shelter for cover, eventually emerging to brave the long climb on the semi-urban A-road. Once at the top it was a long descent to the town of Eastleigh. The main road seemed to run to the east of the town centre, parallel to the railway lines. Finding the actual centre was a bit of a challenge, but once there; it had the feel of a 'new town.' So I did what anybody would do in such a place and headed for McDonald's.

As I ate my 'Big Breakfast,' two clinically obese women reminded me that eating too much of the stuff perhaps isn't the best option for staying healthy. Maybe the health authorities had placed them there for this very purpose?

I then got on a bit of a mission, completing the remaining miles to the M27 motorway and picking up the road it was built to replace – the A27. This was an undulating affair with a semi-urban feel, like a roller coaster ride through suburbia. I passed a boat-filled marina and then paused for a chocolate 'Yuk' milk drink as the road headed skyward again.

"What is this *Yuk*?" I hear you ask.

Well, we are trying to avoid brand names as much as possible, and as most of these drinks have names beginning with the letter Y, 'Yuk' fits the bill perfectly.

After this I remember climbing a wooded hill and later plunging back into urbanity, sticking with this road all the way to Fareham, which was perhaps eight or nine miles away. With a 55-minute wait for the train to Brighton I decided to take a look at the town centre, which was just a straight east-west High Street of modest proportions; rudimentary but hardly striking. I found solace in a branch of a familiar pub chain and whiled away the minutes with a pint. 'Beer o'clock' had come early. You could call it 'enforced drinking courtesy of the railways.'

The flip-side of this is when I regularly find myself missing connections on my daily commute home from work. Armed with my pushbike I generally choose to cycle the second part of the journey rather than wait half an hour with the limited choice of lager or cider available at the station. Conversely, I call this 'enforced fitness by the railways.' In fact travelling by train can be a bit like playing 'spin the bottle' – I don't know what to do so I'll let the rail operator decide for me. Maybe that's a niche they could get into – lifestyle advice. I imagine the first bit of advice they'd give me is 'Get a car!'

And with that, we climb back into our time travelling DeLorean and rewind further, to the most blissful April in living memory.

KENNET & AVON CANAL (EAST) AND SHAFTESBURY DROVE

16) Woolhampton Waterside

Right, this is the big one – the longest of any of the trips I had undertaken by bike, and combined with a three-night camp with those friends of mine, I spent a total of seven nights out of eight sleeping outdoors. Such a mission was made possible by an unprecedentedly warm April. Unbeknown to me, my future wife was visiting England for the first time and it would be easy for the weather to give the false impression that our climate was similar to that of Tenerife or Cuba.

I think spring is the best season in England anyway. There are golden fields of rapeseed, as well as pink and white blossom on the trees, woodlands carpeted with bluebells and fresh, light-green leaves. It is like taking a walk through the paint-chart I mentioned in the last chapter. Summer can be nice, but our expectations are all too often raised and then dashed into a million pieces. August, as my grandmother used to say, is usually 'all gust.'

This exploration of the West Country began on a Sunday afternoon and involved that three-mile death-defying dash across London from St Pancras to Paddington. It is when seated on a different looking Great Western train that one gets the sense of embarking upon an adventure. A British couple were occupying two seats that had been reserved by an American couple. I cringed as they protested about having to move. Once again our country was letting the side down and showing us to be a bunch of lazy curmudgeons.

So often I have encountered visitors from other countries who have seen Hugh Grant films and imagine English life to be similar, only for their perceptions to be smashed to smithereens when they arrive and encounter 'British hospitality.' Personally I feel ashamed when we behave in this way. Politeness costs nothing and it's about the only remaining thing we have a reputation for. Let's not squander it, hey?

The train seemed to go on strike about halfway between London and Reading, and when I finally reached the traditional county town of Berkshire I was disorientated. I wanted to find the Kennet and Avon Canal but was struggling.

This 87-mile canal links The Thames at Reading with Bristol and The Avon. If the Grand Union was a forerunner of the M1, this would be a precursor to the M4. Back to the Canal and River Trust website for some info:

The section I was about to ride from Reading to Newbury is the oldest, opening in 1724. Boats could reach Bath from the Bristol end in 1727, but it wasn't until 1810 that the middle section of the canal via Devizes was completed, successfully linking the two. In the 1960s the canal fell into disrepair and some parts became unnavigable, but the Queen officially reopened the route in 1990 and it has been popular ever since. Having asked for directions I eventually located the canal and began my westward pedal.

Having ridden the Thames Path to Reading from London the year before, this seemed a natural continuation of the route, for beyond Reading there isn't much of The Thames that you can cycle, unlike this canal which has a great towpath all the way to Bath. Best of all, the majority of it is hard surfaced, except for around fifteen miles (my estimate based on memory) in the middle before you reach Devizes. When I reached the first lock on the southern fringes of Reading, I paused for a Scotch egg and a drink.

After this I made a mistake, not realising that the main path bridged the river. I continued, until I found my route veering away into a grassy common and then did a U-turn. 'You turn if you want to...' - Hang on, I've done that one already.

To be honest I don't remember a great deal about the seven or eight mile ride to Aldermaston. As I came to a tree-lined section my mobile phone began to ring, giving me an excuse to pause and relax on the bank as I chatted. There was a café at Aldermaston, but I decided to continue to Woolhampton, where there was a pub beside the river with benches outside upon which one can quaff a pint and watch the boats drift by. It was aptly named The Rowbarge.

I decided to sample a walnut, blue cheese and poached pear salad, and the vibes were peaceful as I sat outside. I wasn't going to push it too far today, as it was now tea-time and there's nothing worse than searching for a spot to sleep in darkness, so I took an exploratory wander northward over the bridge to the village centre. Beyond the A4, another lane headed steeply up the wooded hillside, but there was a sufficient air of 'trespassers will be killed' about the area to send me scuttling back to the canal.

Just a few miles north from here is the village of Bucklebury, famous of course for being the former home of the Duchess of Cambridge when she was plain old 'Kate Middleton.'

Returning to the bridge and The Rowbarge, I continued westward along the canal for a short distance until I noticed a large copse to my left. This seemed to have grown up in some marshy land, but it was thankfully dry as I hauled my bike over the weeds to a suitably hidden location. Before long, I was laying in tranquillity, listening for the final bird-call heralding the night. Being a single man at the time, in such surroundings I could imagine that the couples holding hands that I occasionally felt a pang of jealousy towards could feel no more contented than I did at this moment.

In such peaceful surroundings, it is also hard to imagine the monotony of repetitive work, or the cauldron of thoughts that this can stir up, as being part of the same existence. It often seems that the countryside is a natural sedative there for the taking. Could this be the 'big, bright-green pleasure machine' that Simon and Garfunkel used to sing about? Perhaps.

17) Hungerford Horror

A fox woke me up with its eerie cry in the night. This can sound something like a baby crying to the untrained ear. Some deer also ran past me. I could hear trains nearby too, rattling their way through the village between Reading and Newbury.

At 9am, I decided to rise from my slumber and begin another day's pedalling. Negotiating my way out of weeds and back to the canal towpath, I began my day wearing a woolly hat and gloves, but as I wended my merry way towards Newbury, I gradually shed these outer layers. The coat eventually came off too; it was to be a glorious, sunny day.

As I passed Thatcham on the opposite bank, the scenery became a bit industrial, with warehouses and the like. However, Newbury was very pleasant indeed and I left the canal trail to explore the centre. It's most famous facet is surely the racecourse, however, my AA Book of British Towns reveals the little known fact that England's first true factory was established in the town in the 15th century, employing over a thousand wool weavers.

I eventually found a café near an area of parkland and enjoyed an English breakfast with a pot of tea on a seat outside, from which I could admire the canal. I asked a man nearby what was worth seeing in Newbury and he suggested the market square. This was indeed an impressive centrepiece to the town, and as I wandered up the northbound street beyond it I made a quick phone call to cancel a medical appointment. I had decided to continue this ride for as long as I could, so weather permitting, I would not be home in time for any malarkey like that.

With the doctor safely despatched, I returned to my bike feeling even more positive and continued my canal-side ride. The towpath was hemmed in by buildings at the centre of the town, and I recall crossing the main bridge and returning to the canal bank via a narrow, stepped alleyway.

There were some lakes to the north of the canal as I left the town and I remember a lot of small, shrubby bushes in this vicinity. These were a slightly darker green than 'Spring Leaves' on our generic DIY store paint-chart. The scenery was very pleasant and I took a brief pause to sit on a bench by a lock at Kintbury.

Before long I'd reached Hungerford, which seemed a pleasant small town, but for me it was time for a pit stop. I backtracked a bit from the main street to find a quiet pub. I asked the barman if I could fill my water bottle and he directed me to the toilets. This hadn't occurred to me before as I'd always had a notion that bathroom tap water wasn't suitable for drinking, but just because the sink is near a toilet doesn't mean the water is from the toilet I guess! So I filled my bottle and have been doing so ever since.

Returning to the bar, I tried three real ales over the course of two pints. The mathematicians among my readers will have deduced that two of the drinks were halves. I then got chatting to a Scotsman (there's always one wherever you go). I decided to calmly open up a hornet's nest in the way that the TV interviewer Louis Theroux often innocently does.

"The only thing I really know about Hungerford is the massacre," I ventured. The locals then revealed that the killer, Michael Ryan, had drunk in the pub prior to going ballistic and seemed a fairly normal 'run of the mill' guy.

The Hungerford massacre took place in 1987 and 17 people were killed, including Ryan himself. This ranks him as an even more prolific killer than the Yorkshire Ripper (13 victims) and Jack the Ripper (who was said to be responsible for 11 murders), although Thomas Hamilton, the Dumblane killer took the lives of 18 people including himself.

The affable gent in the bar then asked where I was from. This was a tricky question as I had been living a double life, enjoying the urbanity of being close to work at a bedsit in the seaside town of Folkestone whilst returning to my mother's house in a village near Ashford for weekend socialising. Ultimately, the weekend bit won and I moved back to the countryside. However, this gent hadn't heard of either Ashford *or* Folkestone so my answer needn't have been quite so precise.

So, back on the trail, I continued westward, although my pace was beginning to flag a little. The scenery was very rural indeed, with gentle rolling hills beside the canal, and the towpath now in its unsurfaced phase, which generally slows the pace of cycling right down.

I stopped to eat another Scotch egg by a bridge over a stream, and further on near Crofton Mill I had a lay down at the edge of a field filled with dandelions. I then received the customary phone call and wandered around the field-edge behind the hedge as I chatted.

It is strange that some people can happily chat away on their mobiles on a packed train, sharing their sordid anecdotes with the entire carriage, yet for me, making any kind social call is something private, and I think this incessant wandering during calls may be a subconscious attempt to make sure nobody is lurking nearby, listening in.

A chilly breeze made an appearance at this point, and a little way after this I reached the highest point on the canal. Steep, wooded banks surrounded the waterway, and ahead I could see a tunnel – the only significant one on the entire canal. I rode beyond the point where the towpath climbs away steeply from the canal in order to get a closer look, and stood on a floating metal pontoon which was tethered at the side of the canal, enabling myself to see right through.

There is always a sense of disappointment when one is unable to cycle through a tunnel, be it on a canal or one of those converted rail routes. So reluctantly, I went up and over on the pathway, which undulated through woodland and eventually descended to rejoin the canal.

I remember glimpsing downland to the north of the canal, and as I reached Pewsey, there was a wooded embankment at the road bridge. I had decided to camp in the vicinity of the village and now began looking for bushes into which I could dive. There seemed to be a sufficient copse beside the road to the north of the canal, but I'm not too keen on camping near A-roads. A nice, substantial wood was what I really wanted.

About a mile beyond Pewsey one encounters the little hamlet of Wilcot. I was now on familiar ground, for I'd had to end a bike ride from Bath (the opposite end of the canal) the previous summer, due to torrential rain. Today was much more pleasant, and in the interest of synchronicity I headed straight for the pub that had given me solace from the downpour before – The Golden Swan.

However, it wasn't quite 6pm, so I sat outside until the doors opened. When they did, I opted for a pot of tea and got chatting to a couple and a cyclist who, like myself, had ridden from Reading. The strange coincidence was that he had once lived with somebody in the very village where I come from in Kent. Now really, how likely is that when you are around 140 miles away from home?

By the time I left the pub, the temperature was plummeting. I rode the familiar route into Pewsey, which has a one way system near the station. It is a large village which feels more like a small town, and as I came out onto the main street, I quickly located a kebab shop. As it was cold, I asked if I could sit on the large, white window sill to consume my kofte. They obliged.

"What's a kofte?" I hear some of my readers ask. Well, here once and for all is my definitive layman's guide to kebabs.

Kofte – This is a stick of spicy minced lamb cooked on a skewer and decanted into the pitta bread as a long, thick strip. This was my weapon of choice today.

Doner – thin strips of lamb shaved off of a huge rotating cylinder of meat. This is the one that punters usually opt for when spilling out of the pub at midnight; it's quick, it's simple and it satiates the desire for immediate calorific intake. Available in 'chicken' too.

Shish – cubes of lamb cooked on a skewer. More healthy than the doner as it's pretty much pure meat. However, some patience is required while it cooks. Also available in 'chicken'.

Shashlik – the connoisseur's 'shish' really, as this has the same cubes of lamb but augments them with green peppers, onions, mushrooms, etc. My personal favourite.

House special – also known as 'the abattoir' - this is the entire oeuvre of the kebab shop slammed in an almighty piece of pitta bread. Basically all of the above and then some.

Having eaten my delicious evening meal, I ventured back into the now-quite-bracing cold, and headed back up the lane towards Wilcot. I had already spotted my 'campsite,' for there was a wood on the right-hand-side of the lane as I climbed back up the hill. I surreptitiously dived into the trees, and before long I was gazing up through the branches, snug within a warm sleeping bag, as the stars began to twinkle in the heavens.

I cast my thoughts back over the day, and the most interesting thing I'd learned seemed to be about the life-cycle of salmon, which I'd gleaned from an information board at a point where the River Kennet meets the canal. Special conduits had been made to allow the salmon to swim upstream here, because the salmon is born in shallow water, then it swims towards the sea, before making its way back upstream to breed and die.

This struck me as not too dissimilar from the 'standard model' of human life. You're born, you explore a bit, then you return to your familial area to pass on your genes to another generation who are supposed to do exactly the same. It all sounds rather banal when you look at it that way, but then I guess that's why they invented cycling and camping.

18) Salisbury's Steeple

A pheasant kept making a noise and fluttering its wings in the early hours of the morning. I mean, what is the point of doing that when somebody is trying to sleep?

The day began with a ride back into Pewsey, initially to use the lavatory in the railway station. Then I found a bakery in the centre and opted for a cup of tea, a pasty and delicious French horn filled with jam and cream, like my grandmother used to bake. I sat outside at a round table beneath an awning beside the pavement. Then it was time to face the music and ride.

I headed south on the A345 road out of Pewsey, which soon brought me to the village of Upavon. The settlement is located on the southward flowing River Avon, not to be confused with the 'Avon' that gives the canal its name, well half of its name at least. No, *this* Avon flows down through Salisbury and Ringwood to emerge into The English Channel at Christchurch Harbour. My logic was that following the river would mean lots of easy, flat riding. How wrong I was!

At Upavon, I turned left and then right onto a lane which took me via Enford and a series of small villages. There was a height barrier coming across from the pub and I realised that I was entering a militarised area. As I continued, there were tank crossing points and one village had the feel of a settlement that had been created purely to house troops and their families. In other words it was hardly touristic.

The open fields rolled in expansive curves, and if I looked across the valley I could see the A-road undulating on the other side of the river, so this option wouldn't have been any flatter, making me feel better about my choice of route.

I remember a semi-urban feel to the village of Bulford where I crossed a main road. The lane climbed steeply beyond this, back into pastoral farmland. I was getting an early morning workout whether I liked it or not.

Next I descended to bridge the mighty A303 – 'Highway to the Sun' as one author proudly bestows it in his literary homage to the road. I only know of one other A-road that has its own book, this being 'A272 – Ode to a Road.' What is it about these east-west A-roads that so inspires writers? Are they trying to create the same kind of mythology around these routes as America's most famous highway, Route 66?

And so I descended to the small town of Amesbury; far less famous than the structure on the hillside above it – Stonehenge.

Not too far away is Woodhenge, where concrete markers replace the six concentric rings of wooden posts which it is thought may have once supported a building. A historian at my workplace informs me that the two structures need to be viewed together; wood, to represent life, and stone to represent death.

In order to steer myself towards the 'wood' side of things I decided to satiate my hunger. I popped into a shop in one of the town's central streets and emerged with a raw jelly, a pork and egg pie and an expensive bottle of tonic water. Without wishing to savage the place, I found the centre of Amesbury fairly unremarkable, but OK nonetheless.

It was then time for my three-mile detour to Stonehenge. The westward road out of the town presented me with a steady climb. As I neared the dual carriageway A303 bypass I could see cars queuing where the road 'singled' to reach the roundabout at least half a mile beyond. I understand that the road layout has since been altered here, with the road that branched off of the 'Highway to the Sun' being erased from existence, a bit like the careers of those dodgy TV presenters I mentioned much earlier.

Thankfully there was a pathway beside the A303 at this point, and although not strictly legal for cyclists, I viewed this as my safest option. I crossed the roundabout to take the former A344 towards this Mecca. This was bounded by imposing wire fences on both sides, making it feel more like I was back on military ground than nearing a national treasure.

I tentatively surveyed the entrance which was thronging with people, and weighed up the odds of paying the £7.50 entry fee or just gazing at the stones through the wires. The gaze won.

It is always my bugbear that a stone monument has existed here in some form or another for around 4,500 years and as far as we are aware nobody ever tried to extract cash for people to view it until the latter part of the 20th century, so I wonder why this fee has been necessary for less that 1% of its existence, especially given that visitors are completely free to walk round and touch the similarly ancient stone circle at Avebury without even opening their wallets (although the pub at the centre no doubt achieves this aim voluntarily).

Ok, we'd better have some facts:

Stonehenge began its existence as an earthwork which dates back to around 3,000BC. The next stage is estimated to be around 2,500BC when sarcen stones and bluestones were erected to form a monument. The sarcen stones were probably from nearby Marlborough Downs but the smaller bluestones were transported all the way from the Preseli mountains in South-West Wales. The monument was completed by around 1,500BC.

The first major restoration of the monument took place in 1901. It is interesting to view photographs that predate this era to see the collapsed appearance of many of the stones; quite alien to the Stonehenge we know now and often mistakenly assume to have been the same for thousands of years. At one point there were even buildings near to the henge.

And so, after a brief stare through the wires, I returned towards Amesbury, but turned right off of the former A303, to continue my southward jaunt down the Avon Valley. The unclassified road undulated quite a lot, as wooded headlands nosed their way up against the meandering river, but eventually things levelled out a bit as I reached 'The Woodfords' – Upper, Middle and Lower to be precise. These villages were familiar from the 2006 hike from Kent to Somerset, where I had stomped off up the hillside to the west of the lane with my accomplice Tom, as we doggedly followed the Monarch's Way footpath. It was now 'beer o'clock' without a doubt.

I stopped at a pub called The Wheatsheaf and sat outside in the beer garden, returning to the bar twice more, thus consuming three different ales over the course of 2.5 pints. Some people from New Zealand eventually chatted to me and I could have easily stayed for another pint, as the atmosphere was positively tranquil, verging on idyllic.

After this I made my way to Old Sarum, another ancient relic, but this time a huge mound which was an Iron Age hill-fort. I walked around the southern edge which provided great views down to Salisbury below. This young upstart of a city superseded Old Sarum when the cathedral was moved there in 1226. I wandered through the ruins and then ate some chocolate digestives to augment the historic vibes (quite logical really).

Interestingly Old Sarum was officially uninhabited by the 19th century and became known as a 'rotten borough,' for it still had representation in parliament. These rotten boroughs were anywhere where somebody could secure power and influence in parliament with just a handful of votes. Politics in general seems to be heading that way these days with apathy reigning supreme, but anyway I digress.

It was an easy cruise down the A345 into Salisbury, and I headed straight for the cathedral, which has the UK's tallest church spire at 404 feet. However, this was never the tallest building in the world. Lincoln Cathedral held this epithet from 1311 to 1548 when its 525-foot central spire collapsed.

Salisbury Cathedral also contains the world's oldest surviving working clock, which dates from 1386AD – basically a jumble of cogs with no face, because in this era clocks merely chimed the hours with a bell. And if this wasn't enough for you, Salisbury Cathedral houses one of only four surviving copies of the Magna Carta too.

After taking in all these ancient vibes I headed for the default option 'pub chain' and enjoyed a curry, complete with poppadom, naan bread and chutney, washed down with a cup of tea. I then ordered a second cup and sat outside. A friend texted me and reminded me of Peter Gabriel's song 'Solsbury Hill,' which both of us had always misheard as 'Salisbury.' This would have no doubt buzzed through my head for the rest of the day.

I felt quite tired as I left the pub and headed off south-westward on Old Blandford Road, which took the form of a long, dead straight climb that I pursued on foot. Towards the end of this road a track veered off to the right, neatly meaning that I didn't have to ride on the main A354. This was the Old Shaftesbury Drove; a drovers' road merely being a track used by farmers to move livestock on foot from one place to another. Whilst in the city, I'd popped into a branch of a large book outlet to peruse the local Ordnance Survey sheet, which is where I serendipitously noticed this enticing off-road line leading exactly where I wanted to go. Altogether now: 'How good is that?'

At the beginning of the route a gypsy guy who had moved here from Kent began chatting to me. I talked a bit about Kent and asked him if there were any places to camp along the route. He said that there were plenty of copses along the way and he seemed to know my home area quite well too.

The trail then climbed steadily, with a horse racing course below me to the right. Once at the top, things flattened out as the route pressed on westward, through woodlands. It had a similar feel to the western half of The Ridgeway which I had cycled the year before.

There was a field with a lot of tin sheds in, and I seemed to be upon the middle of three parallel east-west ridges. Then after a few miles, the trail passed through more trees, and as always I did a little recce on the area before committing to camping. I wandered off to the left of the path and found a spot where I could secrete myself behind the bushes, close to the fence bounding the copse from the open farmland which sloped away with the hill.

There was time for a phone call, and then dusk fell and the zeds began to drift into the night sky once again. Zzz...

19) Shaftesbury Nostalgia

Shaftesbury had been on my 'to do list' for many years. As a child, family holidays took me to most corners of the mainland coastline courtesy of strategically located Haven camps containing rows of white chalets and caravans. Then later on, a challenge to visit every lighthouse in England and Wales with my father pretty much completed the seaside for me. But there were many gems deep within the English countryside that I had yet to visit, this one not least because of the boy pushing his bike up Gold Hill in the 1970s Hovis bread advert to the strains of Dvorak's New World Symphony.

It was the strains of a tractor that woke me up however, and when one is out of doors ensconced within a sleeping bag, such vehicles often sound as though they are going to plough straight over you. Now roused, a man ambled past on the trail as I stuffed everything back into my rucksack. Once on my bike, I soon overtook him, and as I rounded a curve a magnificent view revealed itself on my left – a series of hilly ridges jutting their way across the valley, with their bright springlike shades of green (remember our paint-chart?) enhanced by the early morning sunshine.

There is always a real freshness in the air when cycling on sunny mornings such as this. However, I was surprised when the track began to rapidly descend from the ridge, winding its way downward towards the A30. Had I lost the Old Shaftesbury Drove?

At the bottom, I asked a man approaching a junction in his car and discovered that I had indeed reached the end of 'the drove' and that Shaftesbury was about five miles along the A30 from here. 'No challenge,' I thought, as I began to pedal westward with the end of the ridge of hills to my left, although I felt a little cheated that the Old Shaftesbury Drove didn't actually make it as far as Shaftesbury. The Old Middle of Nowhere Drove might be a better name.

Yet this route surprised me in being something of a slog. I'm not sure if it's one of those deceptive roads which look flat but are steadily climbing, or if I was just beginning to feel fatigue after three days of cycling. Maybe both, for Shaftesbury stands on a high ridge with spectacular views in all directions.

My first port of call was a café for the all-essential cup of tea. This central area at the top of the famous hill is awash with tourism and reminded me a little of some of the small towns in Bavaria. I then made the legendary descent down Gold Hill, with its steep, cobbled street and quaint, thatched cottages. The part you don't usually see is where it reverts into a normal tarmac road with parked cars at the bottom. This would have shattered the illusion on the advert somewhat.

From here I walked up some steps to an area known as The Promenade, which is a pathway running west around the top of the hillside, adorned with public gardens. I rounded Castle Hill, and from here the fantastic views switched to the northward direction. I remember seeing four young ladies, all sitting alone admiring the view. This seemed uncanny, as prior to this I had been musing that you don't often encounter women on their own engaging in these outdoor pursuits. I had postulated that in our culture men may feel more free to follow such whimsical interests. I had clearly got this wrong at Shaftesbury.

Being single at the time, I used to notice that seeing a woman out for a drink on her own in a quiet country pub was as rare as spotting a dodo, not that I would have said anything if I had spotted any potential dates. Authors of cycling narratives are far too shy for that kind of thing. Thus, those hoping to meet somebody special are coerced into going to nightclubs where everybody has to shout and ends up appearing equally 'Neanderthal.' Well, right or wrong, that's how it felt at the time. Such notions really didn't matter at all now, as I sat, admiring the view myself for a good ten minutes before concluding that I had 'done Shaftesbury.'

I concluded that it was all a bit too bustling and touristy for me to hang around for a lunchtime pint. I was now set on finding a quiet pub where the bar staff might chat a bit and a few locals might be popping in for a beverage halfway through the working day. So I headed northward out of the town on the A350 which seemed, unsurprisingly, to be mostly downhill. I diverted off to the left when I reached village of East Knoyle, which is the birthplace of Sir Christopher Wren (you know, the bloke who designed St Paul's Cathedral).

The young barmaid was chatty and came from Gillingham (this is 'gill' as in part of a fish and not as in the imperial measure of capacity, which is how you pronounce the first syllable of the much larger town in Kent of the same name).

I enjoyed a bacon and stilton baguette and recalled passing through the nearby hamlet of West Knoyle when hiking from Kent to Somerset in 2006. With such nostalgia in mind, I decided to head back along some of that hallowed route. I undertook a steep, leafy climb on a lane north-eastward and passed what looked like a disused railway tunnel. Then it was a long descent to the village of Hindon.

This pleasant place with tree-lined streets at the centre hadn't changed a lot in the years that had passed since two stick-wielding, Moses-like hikers had passed through, and soon I was heading east along the B-road, passing the scattered houses of Berwick St Leonard, just slightly downhill in a valley to my left.

Next was Fonthill Bishop, where a small farm shop that I had popped into during that epic hike had now bitten the dust. I took a left turn to climb out of the valley and up to the A303. The lane curved repeatedly as the hills rolled all around, and soon I had reached the 'Highway to the Sun.' It was in dual carriageway mode at this point, but there was a concrete track running parallel heading east. As I pounded my way up this shadeless hill, the searing heat hit me. It felt like I was sweating blood!

To make matters worse I suddenly realised that this drive wasn't taking me where I wanted to be; I needed to be on the trail around a quarter of a mile further south. I made an executive decision to cut across the fields (not something I make a habit of), and I recall coming up past farm buildings and eventually finding the semi-overgrown trail, which descended eastward behind a line of trees. Shade at last!

The state of footpaths, bridleways and byways has always frustrated me. Admittedly they are rarely the essential routes that they were prior to that advent of the motor car, but if I see a line on a map, I do like to know that it is clear enough for me to pass through without being tripped, stung, scratched or forced to do a U-turn. Following the cuts imposed by David 'Scissorhands' Cameron and chums, clearing such routes was no doubt quite low in the hierarchy of jobs at the time. In fact, the only things *not* being cut in that era were the weeds.

As a result, councils often enlist voluntary 'rights of way' wardens to help out with the clearing work. For many years I was one of these, but upon requesting another batch of yellow, plastic arrows to pin to fence posts, I discovered that policy had been changed and that these could no longer be given out to 'untrained' individuals. For goodness sake - it's not a firearm; it's a plastic marker disc!

This lack of trust in hard-working, unpaid volunteers prompted me to decide that perhaps the council were best equipped to do the work themselves. I felt this sentiment in a 'go forth and multiply' kind of way. So much for the 'Big Society.'

Yet, old habits die hard, and as time passed and the weeds began to reassert themselves in my local area, I found it hard not to trample down the nettles and chunky stems of cow parsley or to wind the snakelike brambles around the wires of the fence to halt their invasion. What was going on? Had the council brainwashed me? I couldn't stop myself from helping them with their work. Maybe the 'Big Society' wasn't nonsense after all. Maybe eventually even the 'fat cat' tax dodgers would feel the pang of guilt and stop hiding their money from the treasury too. Some hope.

Fortunately this particular track became clearer as it climbed back out of the valley. I surveyed a spot where I had camped beside the grassy trackway with my friend Tom, and then climbed, passing scattered bushes to cross a road. Beyond was a familiar lane section entering woodland, where after a series of curves, the trackway settled upon the dead straight course of the old Roman road which headed from the Severn Estuary to Salisbury.

Halfway along this Roman section there is a left turn to descend to Great Wishford if you so desire, but I continued directly ahead, on the ancient route which streaked purposefully through tall, evergreen trees. I rested on a log as I neared the end of this section and gathered my energies for the descent from Cranbourne Chase and the West Wiltshire Downs to Wilton.

This downhill section ended up with two tracks running parallel, like a kind of ramblers' dual carriageway. Eventually it wound down into the suburbs, for Wilton seems pretty much joined to Salisbury, and I used the A30 and A36 to expediently transport myself back into the cathedral city.

The scenery around the A36 had a parkland feel to it, but lazing in the greenery or even stopping to take in the historic vibes were not on my mind. I wasted no time and headed straight back out, northward, on the slowly climbing A345, bouncing away from the city centre like a pinball hitting a cushion. This road was familiar ground, for it had marked my triumphant freewheel into the city yesterday, down from the earthworks of Old Sarum. It already felt like a lifetime ago.

It was a suburban Co-op shop that eventually enticed me off of my bike, and I emerged with a bottle of Lucozade, some cake, and to be healthy, a pot of olives. It was now about 6pm and the route for my final five or six miles was set in stone in my mind. I would make my way back up to Old Sarum and then attempt to follow the Roman road towards Winchester, camping in the very same woodlands I had camped with Tom all those years ago. Here you can see the appeal of cycling in a nutshell, for a day's hiking between two camping spots had taken a mere few hours on the bike. The only problem was, I couldn't find the road eastward from Old Sarum.

I ended up skirting the northern fringes of Salisbury's housing estates on a series of paths which definitely weren't Roman. I was lost among the playing fields. I eventually located the Roman road in the form of a lane which led up to the A30 via a steep climb out of the Bourne Valley. The route continued as a byway, and soon the footpath from the Figsbury Ring (Neolithic / late Stone Age circular henge) fed in from the left.

The route beyond was a wooded affair, just to the south of the village of Firsdown. I decided that this might be a nice place to stop for a rest, but my detour into the village proved fruitless. There was just a wide, straight B-road and no sign of a long, cool pint. When I asked an old lady if she could direct me to a pub she looked as though I had just landed from Saturn.

'A pub? A pub in Firsdown? The very thought of it!'

So I concluded that the village must have been as dry as my throat and returned to the Roman trail, which brought me out to a familiar crossroads of lanes. Beyond this the trail 'manned up' to face the foreboding, wooded, hill climb ahead.

Halfway up the ascent, the trail seemed unable to maintain its direct course and was contorted by a few bends. It was around here that I passed the hallowed camping spot, but I had no intention of sleeping until I'd been satiated with a fine, brown beer. I would get this, at last, in Middle Winterslow. There are three 'Winterslows,' imaginatively named *West, Middle* and *East.*

The Roman route emerged from the woodlands, with scattered houses (the kind that come with stratospheric mortgages) surrounded by trees, ushering me into the village. When I reached the lane, I located The Nelson Arms with ease, and before long I was sat outside with that elusive pint. Unable to quash my tendency for exploration, I decided to try out the second pub. This was further along the lane, after it had detoured off of the Roman route to descend a hill.

Another pint later, I concluded that I wasn't going to extract a lot of conversation in either of these alehouses. They seemed to be 'local pubs for local people' at least on this particular night anyway. So, as dusk fell, I headed back from whence I'd came, and once I was suitably deep within the woods, I selected my spot for a good night's kip. This was just at the top of the bank where the trail began to curve downward.

To be honest, it wasn't the most comfortable spot, due to being on a slight incline. A word of warning to any camper is that even the slightest slope will guarantee you a 'Paul Simon' moment (slip sliding away) at least once during the course of a night-time. And nobody wants that. Speaking of the great songwriter, I see that he has since opened up a chain of carpet trading stores.

Owls hooted and when somebody walked past on the trail at 2am, I briefly poised myself for defence. I mean, who goes for a stroll in the woods at that time?

Through the trees in the distance, perhaps two miles away, I could see a set of traffic lights changing from red to green and back in sequence. Presumably these were somewhere way below the ridge on the A30. Anyway, these distant dots of colour had a soothing effect, and before long my eyes were closed and I was entering a dream about being in a Lego-building competition and making a power station complete with a line of pylons out of the bricks, perhaps generating just enough power to keep a set of traffic lights going through the long, dark night.

20) Stockbridge's Scarecrow

Today was to be the final push – to Winchester! Although the target distance of roughly twenty miles was considerably less than the last few days, I would soon find myself struggling to sustain the momentum. In truth, a five-day cycling mission of this kind is something I had never been able to undertake before, and, at the time of writing, have not undertaken since. The reason? The British weather.

Yes, It seems on average that three dry days is about the limit, and having slogged my way through torrential rain during that epic hike in 2006, I was determined not to go for the 'drowned rat' look again. It's not a good look after all.

So it was back onto the Roman road heading east through Winterslow. This descended steeply, and at the bottom I encountered junctions I had not expected. A teenage girl was passing and I asked if she knew where the Roman road went next, naively forgetting that the alignment of Roman roads isn't normally up there in the average teenage mind, which is stuffed full of boy bands and lurid details regarding who's dating who. However, she did get her father who was a bit more clued up about it.

There was another off-road bit, but once returned to tarmac, there was nothing that seemed particularly straight, so I ended up on a trail-like section of the Clarendon Way - a long distance footpath linking Winchester and Salisbury. This eventually descended steeply to the village of Broughton. I had been here before, but as I rode its narrow streets it wasn't firing up any nostalgia neurons.

I'd given up on the Roman road by now and decided to take a look at Stockbridge. There was a long, slowly curving lane to the north of Broughton, leading to the A30. My 'phone a friend' friend rang at this point, which briefly took my mind off of how tough I was now finding it. Every incline suddenly seemed like a mountain.

I turned right onto the A30, which was a typical rural A-road across pastoral farmland, yet the steepness of the descent to Stockbridge surprised me, as did the road's very brief flirtation with dual carriageway.

As you'll remember from an earlier chapter of this book, Stockbridge is a large village strung out along a wide, straight high street between two hills. I went into a partly 'open plan' deli type café and opted for the 'posh' smoked salmon and scrambled egg breakfast. The butchery section of the shop was doing brisk business and I wished my own village in Kent had been as enterprising at keeping these traditional trades alive.

However, the notion of salubriousness about Stockbridge is perhaps a relatively recent phenomenon, for I later discovered that many scenes from the classic eighties children's TV show 'Worzel Gummidge' were filmed here and in nearby King's Somborne. The idea of a scarecrow coming to life and dropping straw all over the street before popping into a café and getting into a food fight with a snooty wooden doll called Aunt Sally seemed a million miles away as I dined on smoked salmon. If Worzel and Aunt Sally were to enter here, utter chaos would ensue and the episode would of course end with the entire place being trashed and the pair being unceremoniously booted out.

After a thoroughly good wander and a phone call that I detailed around half a book ago (Judean People's Front?), it was time to face the music, and in a village surrounded by hills, the only way was, unfortunately, up. I'd decided to reach Winchester via the road formerly known as the A272. This is another one of those illogical redesignations. Allow me to explain.

The bulk of the A272 is a scenic east-west drive across deepest Hamsphire and Sussex, but this section to the west of Winchester has been amputated and reclassified as a B-road. The A272 has instead commandeered a rather aimless link from Winchester to the A30 as its finishing flourish – part of another Roman road, completely unrelated to the rest of the A272.

Whatever you choose to call the road (and I imagine its been called worst things than 'B3049'), the climb from Stockbridge was something of an epic. I was surprised at just how hilly Hampshire can be. What's more, the heat was now searing again and before long I was scuttling beneath a sprawling tree by the side of the road for some shade.

In my mind I was seeking a repeat of two days ago when I stopped in Lower Woodford; specifically a few beers, sitting outside a quiet country pub with interesting small talk from random strangers. I decided that my best bet for such criteria was to detour off to the scattered village of Sparsholt along a narrow lane. The pub I came to was called The Plough, and as I sat outside in the beer garden, a lady and her son did indeed talk to me. They were waiting for somebody to return with an Allen key for some undisclosed reason.

Yet, this didn't quite have the serendipitous feel of the other day. I suppose deep down, I knew that the mission was nearing an end. After my pit stop, I encountered more hills further along the lane. My tyre was beginning to flag too now, and I stopped to pump it back up before the final handful of miles. I did another pinball style rebound when I reached Hampshire's county town, for no sooner had I reached Winchester than I was on a train heading for London – the first leg of my journey home.

That night I would sleep in a real bed, which always feels like the height of decadence after these trips, but this was for one night only, for the following day meant meeting my friends at our local 'glamping' woods, for more fun and mayhem.' All in all, I slept outdoors for seven out of eight consecutive nights. Take that and party!

Oblique reference alert: This is the title of British boy band, Take That's first album. I'm not a fan, but the title is very useful as a smarmy statement meaning 'how good is that?' – a polite alternative to making that 'L for loser' sign with your hand on your forehead.

Before we move on, this seems an opportune moment to tell you a bit more about these luxury camps, for if my cycling trips are the 'yin,' these camps with friends are surely the 'yang.'

The camp is basically a glade in a small private woodland, reached via a narrow path from the nearby public forest, so arriving at the spot has a feel of entering another world, like a tiny grotto hidden from civilisation.

With tents set up and the pit for the fire dug, the friends initiate the camp with the 'first crack.' This has got nothing to do with cocaine, but is merely the act of yanking off the ring pull on the first can of beer of the weekend – the single moment that seems to release a tidal wave of pleasure from the dam, flooding across the whole weekend. From that moment onward, time seems to accelerate, until the ceremonial closing of the gate at the end of the camp when we go our separate ways and start preparing ourselves mentally for the more mundane 'real world' stuff like working.

The two brothers I camp with like to think of themselves as men of the bush, armed with airguns and occasionally shooting a rabbit for a tasty treat (sorry, pet lovers). However, the first meal usually involves a trip to the nearby town of Tenterden for a Chinese take-away. Ray Mears, eat your heart out!

Then the fire is lit and our evening of culture and music begins, courtesy of a small iPod docking station, the function of which is more like a duelling sword, as we each try to outdo the others with our musical selections. From this point on, the conversations get increasingly bizarre and at some point always involve the phantasmagorical notion that a gaggle of young girls are making their way up to the wood armed with more supplies.

At some point the younger of the two brothers usually throws some plastic on the fire and receives a stiff reprimand from his older sibling who, like me, isn't that keen on inhaling carcinogens.

The second day usually commences with a light breakfast, after which the two brothers pop home to collect some meat and avoid having to dig a hole in the ground to do what bears are reputed to do in the woods. Left alone, the Dark Lord of Horror (my friend who specialises in gruesome novels) and I speculate as to whether they are 'cheating' by having a nice, warm shower. Of course, they fiercely deny using products containing 'hydro action liposomes' or any of those other pseudo-scientific terms they use in adverts to try to confuse us into buying beauty products.

The afternoon involves lunch, collecting wood for another rip roaring fire, an occasional walk around the forest and some kind of competition. One such game involves throwing horseshoes over a stick. Apparently they got the idea from a Kings of Leon video – I told you they were serious fans!

As evening falls, the older brother (the 'godfather of campfire cuisine') cooks us a hearty meal, which is served with our first glass of wine of the weekend. The sun sets in an orange burst across the nearby field, and then the first night is repeated, but scaled up to the max with a midnight feast. By the end of the night, the soporific effect of staring into the flames can tend to blur all the angles and one occasionally gets the strangest sensation of being in a completely different place. I understand that some people misuse illicit substances to achieve similar effects. Surely it's much cheaper and healthier just to light a fire and gaze into the flames for six hours?

Beyond this zenith of woodland merriment, we come back down to earth, often heading for our tents as dawn breaks, with the chorus of birdsong lulling us off to sleep. All that remains is a calorific breakfast baguette and then the sorry business of carrying all the stuff out to their Land Rover and closing that ceremonial gate.

To some folk, this description may sound enticing, while others will remain unmoved, but you could say that this particular set of eight days was a pivotal point in appreciating both kinds of camping.

I once read that life can be viewed pretty much like a banquet, with starter, main course and dessert all arriving in due time. I had expected the long hike to Somerset that I undertook in

2006 to mark this transitional point between what I felt was the starter and the much anticipated main course, but in hindsight I think this particular week with it's double-whammy of camping was perhaps nearer the mark. The main course is that point when you feel that your life has actually arrived, rather than that you are still preparing for it, whatever 'it' may be. Of course, you hope it will be a long course, for the dessert is when you start winding down and preparing to push up the daisies. There's no time for cheese and biscuits in *this* banquet – there's not even (as John Cleese said in Monty Python's 'Meaning of Life') a 'waffer-thin mint' at the end of it all.

So now we're going to dig back further to the preceding summer, when the notion of a few days away cycling seemed less like an adventure and more like a 'prescription' therapeutic break from mundaneness and repetition. Let's fire up our time travelling DeLorean once again and plunge further back through the mists of time.

KENNET & AVON CANAL (WEST)

21) Beautiful Bath

The five-day mission just depicted was really 'unfinished business,' for we now rewind to the previous August to my first attempt at cycling the Kennet and Avon Canal. As with so many trips, I set off on the super-duper high speed train to London and faced the task of riding from St Pancras to Paddington. This time I decided to use the towpath of Regent's Canal between the two termini.

This canal is an 8.5-mile link from Limehouse Basin and The Thames in the east of London to just north of Paddington where the Grand Union Canal takes over, running all the way to The Midlands. I had cycled the entire length of Regent's Canal on my 34th birthday. When cycling from end to end, one will encounter three tunnels (two occurring almost together), so one has to negotiate a few backstreets at these points to link the estranged sections of towpath. A good street map is recommended.

St Pancras is roughly the mid-point of the route. As an aside, I always muse that international rail passengers emerging from the UK's second longest mainline rail tunnel from Stratford (the longest being on the same line east of Stratford) aren't being treated to a particularly impressive entry into the European Union's largest city. The view is of a kind of wasteland with scattered construction projects. The journey in on the old mainline from Kent is more rewarding to the eye, with views across to the towering offices of The City and Docklands, before gracefully passing over The Thames to Charing Cross.

Anyway, I joined the canal and headed west, passing the lively throng of Camden Lock (the market used to be great for purchasing 'unreleased' albums by your favourite artists). Beyond this, the canal is bounded by London Zoo. The 'money good, cycling bad' brigade seemed to have strengthened their stranglehold on the towpath since my previous visit, as I recall locked gates at one point and being thrust up onto the road instead. Just to compound this, I was then doused in a light shower. I'm sure there had been an option to push your bike along the towpath via Little Venice when I rode the route before.

I eventually reached Paddington and settled for the culinary delights of Burger King. My 'phone a friend' friend rang as I prepared to board my Great Western train to Bath. He seemed a little green with envy as I embarked on another random mission, wishing to do something similar himself, at the time being married and happily settled with the social life of a pensioner (I'm sure he won't mind me saying this as he said it himself).

I felt great anticipation as my train streaked westward to Reading and Swindon. There is always something nice about heading west (or north) from London. To those of us shoe-horned into The South-East it feels like venturing out into a vast unknown – in short, a proper holiday.

Clouds cast shadows on the downland as I neared Swindon and gazed southward, across to the North Wessex Downs. Then tiredness crept in, and I found myself nodding off in a strange way where I noticed the sound of the rush of the train disappear for the briefest moment and then return each time, deducing that I had had some kind of micro-sleep. Consciousness is a peculiar thing to analyse. It's hard to keep your eye on the ball when you *are* the ball.

Those who are familiar with the TV comedy 'Only Fools and Horses' will know what I mean by 'Trigger's broom.' The joke was along the lines of, "He's had had the same broom for thirty years. It's had ten new handles and eight new brush-heads." So the philosophical argument is, 'Is it the same broom?' Most people would say 'no,' but when you think about it the human body and mind are not so different.

Both are in a constant process of renewal, and I have heard that there will not be a single atom in your body that was part of you five years ago, so are we the same people that we used to be? Or are we really just a new machine running to an old computer program stored in our ever-changing braincells? Of course we will never know the answer to this, as all our thoughts and memories remain intact, and these are all we have to know who we are. This is a quandary akin to the science fiction scenario of 'teleportation'.

The idea is that you step into a machine which analyses you, before destroying you and recreating an exact replica in a different location. If such a thing ever existed, I wonder if my consciousness would instantly transfer to the new me, or if I would simply cease to perceive anything while the new me seamlessly carries on with all my thoughts and memories and therefore no sense of being a new being. Funnily enough, I explored this dilemma in one of my short fiction stories, which can be easily tracked down for purchase if desired. In the spirit of the BBC, I must point out that I am merely raising awareness here and that this does not constitute advertising, product placement or a shameless plug.

Now, when I alighted at Bath, I decided to savour the city, for I had visited before, but my main aim at *that* time had been to get out onto the cycle route to Bristol as soon as possible. Today, I took time to sit and enjoy a cup of tea in a square near the abbey and listen to the young musicians performing nearby, demonstrating some rather impressive guitar playing.

I then wandered up the hill and found the Royal Circus and Royal Crescent, two neatly rounded, regal looking, Georgian residential projects; the latter being sited at a viewpoint above a substantial area of lush, green parkland. I resisted Bath's prime tourist trap however, this being the Roman baths. The aim of these trips is always to keep costs minimal, so any tourist attraction which costs over a fiver to enter usually gets the heave-ho.

After a visit to Marks and Spencer's, it was time to start my ride and head east, in search of the Kennet and Avon Canal. The canal actually begins its 87-mile course further west in Bristol. However, I was headed eastward, and having located the canal, I passed through two short tunnels, something that one rarely gets to do on a bike, as the towpaths usually disappear during subterranean sections.

The canal began heading north, climbing via a succession of locks, and slowly curved east and then southward, being raised above the Avon Valley, ever to my left. Narrowboats lined its banks in this highly touristic section.

I eventually reached an impressively high aqueduct. At the age of 35 this was a new experience for me. Believe it or not, I'd lived for all that time without ever seeing an aqueduct or even knowing where you'd go to find one. All I knew of the existence of such structures was the famous quote from Monty Python's 'Life of Brian' which ran along the lines of:

"What have the Romans ever done for us?"

"The aqueduct?"

The view, as the canal suddenly turns eastward to stride over the River Avon, is very satisfying indeed. The canal then followed the river once more before deciding it had had enough of this and crossed it once again. Aqueducts are clearly like buses – you wait your whole life for one and then two come along at once.

It wasn't far beyond this that the scenery began to resemble parkland, with Bradford-on-Avon just to the north. I decided to come off of the towpath by a quaint looking café type area and head into the town to explore. This is of course a euphemism for 'find a pub and sup a pint of some kind.'

Bradford had the feel of a large village more than a small town, although it's population of over 9,000 belies this. The town had been something of an economic powerhouse in the past, with around thirty woollen mills using water and steam from The Avon to power the looms. In the late 19th century, the industry moved northward to Yorkshire and it was clear that Bradford had passed its industrial heyday.

It was a quiet, shady hotel-bar that I frequented now, and as usual I made use the solitude to write up a little bit of the diary that I am now using as a memory aid for this book. After supping up my Guinness, I returned to the canal and the scenery really flattened out as I continued eastward. It was nice to get away from the sound of traffic though, and the canal passed uneventfully through farmland.

The sun came out, and I recall passing some caravans and then pausing to sit on a concrete block and eat some Mediterranean tomatoes and mozzarella. However, without the 'in yer face' views and spectacular construction features, thoughts began to nibble at the edges of my mind, for in these days the primary function of these trips was as a kind of 'chill out.'

At this particular time I had made a friendship with a seemingly pleasant young lady in a 'live music and independent ale' orientated pub in a small town near my home. She had invited me to a festival and declared her present relationship to be moribund. Having enjoyed a genial chat, I imagined this to be the beginning of something good, but in hindsight I wonder if she had struck up the friendship merely to pique her partner of yore. If this was the case, the plan clearly worked, as I believe they are now married. Now, that's about as close to 'scandal' as you're going to get in this book. It's not the Daily Sport after all.

Anyway, the 'will she, won't she' nature of the whole situation began to creep into my consciousness as I rode towards Devizes, like the slime oozing around the edges of a closed door in a horror film. This 'hamster wheel' of thought was fortunately alleviated by the impressive flight of 16 locks at Caen Hill, which form the most impressive part of a set of 29 locks strung out over two miles.

The locks have a uniformity about their spacing, as do the large ponds to the north of each one. It was as if some computer whizz had 'copied and pasted' these pairings all the way up the hillside. The uniformity that I would come to hate in Milton Keynes had a delightful quality here.

As I reached the top, I looked back into the setting sun as it glimmered across the canal and locks, which now appeared like an endless line, giving a similar effect to one of those illusions where you put two mirrors opposite each other to make the nested identical images streak away *ad infinitum*.

Turning around to face the dusk, I continued through quite a deep wooded cutting to the north of the small town of Devizes. I was hoping to check out this historic little place the next day, but for now twilight was imposing its will, so my most pressing concern was to find a place to kip.

I veered away from the towpath on a lane and noticed a byway climbing southward over a large, open hillside. I pummelled my way along this conduit and soon spotted a square of woodland to my left. Taking the next available left turn, I stopped at the closest point to the woodland and climbed over the barbed wire fence to walk across the field and enter the trees to do a 'recce.'

I liked what I saw, and returned for my bike, lifting it over the fence and wheeling it into the thicket. I then laid out my tarpaulin beneath the crepuscular canopy of branches, and satisfied that my bed for the night was good, I wandered back up the slope and stared out of the trees at the brightly shining moon. Tranquillity had been restored, and I returned to my sleeping bag and climbed in, snug as bug in a rug. Life was good.

22) Pewsey Pelt-down

I felt that I had slept well, safely hidden by a fallen tree trunk that I'd laid out my tarpaulin next to. I bundled everything back into my rucksack and emerged from the woodland like a rabbit gazing out of its hole. Lifting my bike back over the barbed wire fence to the trail, I then retraced my route back to the canal.

Devizes is slightly bigger than Bradford and is not to be overlooked, with its castle, market place and apparent concentration of almost 500 listed buildings, but sadly for me the town itself remains on my 'to do' list, for the pitter-patter of rain had started, so I needed to cover some miles along the canal swiftly. I understood that the inclement weather would be sweeping in from the west. Could I really outrun the weather? In truth, I doubted it. All I could do was clock up as many miles as I could before running for cover.

The gravel surface of the towpath soon ended and I followed a worn line through the grass. I was now on that central section of the route which is clearly deemed too remote to surface.

The rain gradually became more persistent, and I sheltered beneath a red, brick bridge to eat a jar of olive mix. The rain made stair-rods on the surface of the canal and a narrowboat slowly approached. The hum of a nice, warm engine got louder and I felt a pang of jealousy that the impending downpour could not impede the pleasure of the canal on a boat, unlike with my two-wheeled exploration. The 'pilot' said hello as he passed and I asked him where I was, for this truly felt like the middle of nowhere.

A little further along the towpath I remember passing a large, brick pub standing alone beside the canal. I wandered round to the front door, but alas, it was closed.

The next outpost of civilisation along the canal was the village of Wilcot. The incessant precipitation was beginning to carp on a bit by now, and all pleasure was rapidly draining from this endeavour. It had become a gutty slog.

At Wilcot Bridge, I pounded southward along the lane, with jets of spray coming up from my wheels. I soon found a smaller, quaint looking pub. To quote The Doors, the time to hesitate was through, there was no time to wallow in the mire – I immediately abandoned my bike outside and went in for a pint. How long would I have to shelter here? Oh what a chore that would be!

Feeling snug and smug, I browsed the newsletters on the walls which made me aware of some of the local issues. There seemed to be a 'villagers versus boaters' thread to some of this, and whilst any antisocial behaviour on the waterway should of course be tackled, I wondered if the perceived inconvenience could have been offset by the additional money that the canal lovers might put into the local economy.

I'm afraid I have seen far too much 'us and them' thinking in village life first hand, and I recall the pandemonium that bordered on village warfare when somebody proposed opening a useful fish and chip shop at my own village in Kent. Anybody would have thought the plan was for a biological weapons plant with all the scaremongering that was going on.

Picture the scene: You hear blood curdling screams and run to the window to view what on earth is going on, but you are unable to see through the river of blood and chip fat cascading down the pane. You open your front door to a scene of carnage worthy of Dante; cars smashed into cars at delirious angles, metal flying through the air and plumes of black smoke climbing high into the sky. And then, out of the corner of your eye, you see a man fighting for his life at the side of the road, gasping for air as he chokes on a piece of cod.

"I never should have supported that chip shop!" you say, and close the door.

Similar 'doomsday' scenarios were thrust in my direction about proposals for an Indian take away and an expanded doctor's surgery (picture crazed doctors running through the streets in white coats lunging at people with syringes). With such fearful attitudes to useful amenities it's little wonder that most villages are dying. Anyway, I'm sure there's nothing like that going on in Wilcot and I hope the residents and the boating folk are now friends.

I found the barman to be very friendly, and a family from Sussex spoke to me, as did a group of well-spoken locals. This wasn't the stereotypical rural accent I had hoped to hear in this area, but the conversation was pleasant nonetheless. Several people had tried to reassure me that things would dry up later in the day, but I found this hard to believe. The skies were as ashen as ever, so I opted for a second pint in order to assess them further. I believe a third beer was in order too, just to make absolutely sure, but no, the skies were not clearing and the rain was more like an unstoppable monsoon. You can't beat the British summer!

Reluctantly, I had to admit that the mission was over. I was throwing in the towel (which is exactly what I needed), and consequently this is one of only two 'one nighters' in this book. Over the course of these trips, I found that generally three nights is about the normal limit of possible cycling and camping before the weather changes. I think this is a fairly reliable assessment of the climate of Southern England. If I decide to produce a second book including more northerly rides I may just have to bite the bullet and face a bit of rain. 'Man up,' as my friend from the woods might say.

I asked for directions to Pewsey station, and then made a dash for it, up the wooded hill on the lane. When I arrived on the platform, there was a two-hour wait for the next train to London. It appeared that in spite of being a large village, the daytime service had been reduced to a bare minimum. Cuts, cuts, cuts, don't you just love 'em?

I couldn't find the men's toilets, so I took a chance on getting arrested and used the dryer in the ladies' to purge the water from my clothes as I stood with various limbs under the blower at contorted angles. The train finally came, and I sat back and watched the remainder of the canal weaving around beside the railway track beneath a bleak, foreboding sky. I would be back.

I still had the three-mile sprint across Central London to go. There was no messing about with canals this time; I merely gritted my teeth and endured the lashing sheets of rain as I pummelled along London's inner ring road. It felt more like November than August. This was purgatory. The only way out of this watery nadir is to do what we always do...

"Who wants to rewind?"

RIDGEWAY WEST

23) Goring Heights

We don't have to rewind far to get to the next trip – just one month to July, and this took place with a generally relaxed frame of mind. Well, it had to be – I'd opted to travel the long way to Reading via Tonbridge and Redhill to save a few quid by not going into London. If the thought of an eighty-mile journey with a station every four miles fills you with horror, then maybe you'd be better heading into London and doing that little ride to Paddington.

I conveniently used the wait between trains at Redhill to nip out and get some fish and chips. Now, Redhill isn't a place you associate with seafood, being roughly in the middle of the land-locked county of Surrey. In fact the sign on the station declared it to be the home of a well-known High Street optician's, unless I misread it, in which case I should have already gone there.

Anyway, the specific outlet matters not particularly, as ever since that day I've noticed these 'Home of...' signs springing up on railway platforms all over the country. It's amazing that with all the heritage and history that the UK has to offer, the only info that will greet arriving visitors is often the name of a company that has some kind of vague connection to the town.

Well, I eventually found myself at Reading. I whisked my way through the town centre and located the Kennet and Avon Canal.

Having found the waterway, I headed north to where it joins the River Thames. It was quite a pleasant ride, where one can envy the homeowners who open their doors onto this pleasant towpath. When I reached the junction, there was a bridge over the mouth of the Kennet and Avon and an elderly gent stood poised to ask me a question.

He wanted to know where the Kennet and Avon Canal was and if it would be possible to walk it. I informed him that he was standing beside it and that if he wished he could walk it all the way to Bath. However, as I moved away I noticed this fellow ask a woman exactly the same question. I felt rather sorry for him, for it appeared that standing by a canal dreaming up random questions to ask strangers was his only way to secure conversation in the social desert known as 'modern urban life.'

At the time I was living alone in a bedsit, so I could understand how difficult it is to make friends in a new town. I recall saying 'good morning' to somebody who was sitting on my doorstep one morning and receiving that look as though I'd just landed from Saturn or proposed something grossly indecent. Since when was saying 'good morning' the first sign of madness?

With that background I could imagine that in the latter stages of life, the sense of isolation is even harder to take, with most friends and relations now at that big place in the sky. I quite like Paul Simon's song, The Afterlife, where he sings about getting to heaven, only to be asked to 'fill out a form' and 'wait in the line.'

Luckily for me, there was nothing like that required to cycle the Thames Path. I merely pedalled over the footbridge and began my ride westward along the south bank. The hard surfaced path seemed to be sandwiched between the railway line and the river, but eventually I reached a point where wealthy individuals had insisted upon owning the riverbank, so the path was diverted onto the road (A329).

I followed the Thames Path via residential roads and soon found myself deposited back beside the waterway, which made a long, slow curve towards the bridge at Whitchurch-on-Thames.

This is a toll bridge where a lane crosses the river. I rode across to the north side and then headed for the church on my left. Sometimes churches are a nice, cool place to relax and consolidate one's thoughts. This church was reached by some paths around some large, well-to-do houses. It was clear there was no continuation of the Thames Path here, so after popping inside for a few quiet moments, I headed further north along the lane. I then stopped again, having passed a small art gallery on a hill – a serendipitous surprise in a village that is little more than a hamlet.

My favourite exhibit looked like a doll's house, with every surface from the walls to the roof covered with maps of the local area which seemed to fit together perfectly at all vertices. 'How did they do that?' I pondered. Rather than find out, I chatted a bit about my books and cycling trips to the lady presiding over the artwork that day, and then it was time to move on.

The Thames Path dived off to the left and undulated its way through woodland which gradually descended back to the level of the river. I recall passing beneath a railway bridge via some gated meadows. The path was really not intended for cyclists at this point, although I find that if you give way to pedestrians and show respect, generally people can see that you are harmlessly enjoying the countryside, the same as them, and leave you alone.

The only negative experience I've had like this was cycling along the Royal Military Canal Path in Kent. The conversation went something like this as a 'gent' in his sixties wound down the window of his large vehicle as I rode along a gravel track near to the waterway:

"Are you enjoying riding on my drive?"

"I realise that I shouldn't really be cycling but it *is* a public footpath."

"No it's not. This is a private drive."

"I know that there is a footpath for the entire 28-mile length of the canal."

"Well, you're not on it. The grassy section is the path and the gravel is my private drive." (The word 'pedant' came into my mind.)

"OK, I'll go onto the grass."

"Well, If a hundred bikes ride along there it's going to destroy the grass" (I imagine his vehicle weighed about the same as a hundred bikes but I didn't comment).

"I haven't got a hundred bikes though; I've got *one* bike."

There were further mutterings but by that time I'd already made my way up onto the grass and the vehicle then moved away along his precious drive.

Now, had this been a leisure ride, I may well have continued walking until I reached the next rideable section of towpath, but I was on my way to work and time was pressing, so I sneakily got back onto the bike as soon as the vehicle was out of sight and continued, albeit on slightly bumpier terrain than before. What I hadn't bargained for was the vehicle turning around and finding myself subjected to another verbal lashing from a freshly sharpened sexagenarian tongue.

It was at this point that the F-word was introduced into the dialogue ("Hello, Mr F-word!") along with the information that the police would be waiting for me at the other end of that particular section. I imagined an entire unit being scrambled and driven at break-neck speed to the middle of the Kent countryside and laying in the ditch with riot shields awaiting me to come pedalling through, before yelling, 'Get down on the ground!' and firing a few rubber bullets into the air, just to let me know they were serious.

I guess the police were having a busy day as they never showed up, but the conclusion to this whole silly affair is that the Royal Military Canal is the only canal I have encountered where you are expressly not welcome to cycle along the towpath, even if you're respectful. Perhaps this may be because it was never actually used as a towpath, for the waterway was constructed to serve as barrier against a feared invasion by Napoleon, making it the third longest military structure in the UK after Hadrian's Wall and Offa's Dyke. Maybe this anger was just the old defensive attitude of yore resurfacing. So, where were we?

While I made that slight deviation, we have arrived at the village of Goring, where another bridge straddles The Thames.

I had passed myriad yachts as I rode this section. I believe I mentioned before that the wooded hillside to the west of The Thames here gives it a feeling similar to those sections of The Rhine that run through deep gorges. This hill was in fact my first glimpse of the North Wessex Downs, upon which my ride would continue, for the aim of this mission was to ride the western half of The Ridgeway. This ancient trail would take me into deepest Wiltshire and the mysterious village of Avebury. Unlike the eastern section which, as we already know, is quite bitty, this western half is rideable in its entirety. I was pleased about this, as I've witnessed more than enough farmers rupturing their spleens for one lifetime.

But for now I was hungry and in affluent Goring. I stopped in a hotel and ordered a ploughman's lunch which came on a wooden service board. The ploughmen around here were obviously a bit posh. I was very restrained and limited myself to two shandies before the epic climb.

Passing over the bridge to the west side of The Thames I found myself in Streatley, for what appears to be one village is actually two, on opposite banks of the river. I reached the main road and followed it northward until a sign instructed me to turn left. My Ridgeway trail began as a little lane passing a few houses, but it was no use pretending - there was one heck of a climb to come.

When it came, it was in the form of a gravel track, heading in a dead straight line up the hillside. I looked down at the ground and pounded my way skyward. This is a good barometer of a person's general outlook.

Those who like to break up tasks into small stages will tend to look at the ground and glimpse up now and again to assess their progress, while those who like to fix their eyes upon the ultimate goal will stay focussed on the top of the climb all the way through the gruelling ascent.

Upon reaching the summit, I was hoping that the ride would not be as savage as certain sections of the South Downs Way, which seem to bump up and down the hillside a little too often. I was relieved to discover that the western half of The Ridgeway does predominantly stay quite high on the ridge. That said, there was a significant descent and then the trail curved round to the left to climb again, eventually reaching a crossroads of trails where it turned abruptly right to head north-west. Once here, the route is pretty settled, with no massive undulations, at least for the time being.

To my right I could see the stack of fat chimneys at Didcot way below me, occupying the valley like a giant pack of beer-cans. There were little copses now and again, which was a good omen for finding a suitable camping spot, and soon my route was passing underneath the dual carriageway A34. The trail continued unabated, and I remember a lorry being parked in a car park a bit further on.

"So what?" you may say.

Look, it's a book of recollections, right? I didn't say the recollections had to be interesting!

There was also a section where the trail split into two, appearing like a dual carriageway of grassy paths as it climbed the slope ahead. I felt that I was really covering the miles now. However, the sky was becoming cloudy and evening would soon be upon us, so I found an opportune copse that ran along the north side of the path and promptly dived into it.

Just inside I decided to set up a shelter, for this was the first time I had camped using a tarpaulin. As you will know, in later missions I got lazy and generally just dumped the tarp on the ground and kipped on it, but at the moment I was intent on making a proper shelter for myself. It was my 'phone a friend' friend who had leant me his blue fishing tarps, which I now joined together and strung up to the branches to provide a sloping 'roof.'

Having not had this luxurious accessory to carry before, I had devised a method to attach the blue sheet to the crossbar of my bike using loops of string. This too would go out of the window on later trips, when I'd just stuff it into the top of my rucksack. Too much faffing about!

With my shelter erected, I decided to savour the atmosphere and wandered out of the dusky copse onto the trail. Just to the west, The Ridgeway forked to the left and climbed towards the Wantage Memorial, a tall cross which was erected by Lady Wantage to honour Lord Wantage (a.k.a. Robert Loyd-Lindsay) who was one of the founders of the British National Society for Aid to the Sick and Wounded in War, which later became known as the British Red Cross Society.

As I stood by the memorial and admired the view to the north, across the expanses of the Vale of the White Horse leading away below the hills, with those Didcot chimneys ever dominant, I savoured the calm quietness of this isolated spot. The sky was grey and there was a gentle breeze. During the humdrum workday a grey sky can often spark a bad mood, but here, the feeling was completely different. It felt like freedom. It felt like being the king of the hills!

I descended on a path heading northward and then turned 90 degrees right to take the trail that The Ridgeway had forked away from on my ascent - the adjacent side of the original 'fork' if you're into Pythagoras. Soon I found myself back in the woodland. My shelter, bike and sleeping bag were still there and all was good. Beneath the trees the darkness made it feel around half an hour later than out on the trail.

I climbed in and settled down for what seemed to be my cosiest solo camping arrangement ever. It needed to be really, for the weather was about to change.

24) Avebury Encounter

The pitter-patter of rain upon the blue tarpaulin above my head began at about 3am. Safely ensconced in a dry cocoon beneath it, this seemed quite soothing. The next sound I heard was a cacophony of collared doves at dawn – the five-note type, as opposed to the three-note type. I call them all wood pigeons but apparently this is not correct.

I decided to get up properly at 10.30am. It seemed that in these earlier adventures I was more in need of a lie-in. I sat beneath the shelter waiting for the rain to stop. Bearing in mind that the options are very limited beneath a six-foot square, I decided to eat an avocado (as you do), and in the absence of utensils I used the scissors that I had been using to cut the string to secure the tarp to my bike to slice the green fruit in half. I then took a casino membership card out of my wallet and used this as a plastic spoon. I think this is called resourcefulness.

By the time I'd eaten the light green fleshy fruit, the downpour had reverted to drizzle, so I packed everything up and emerged from the trees into a grey haze. With tarpaulin secured and rucksack donned, I headed back up to the Wantage Memorial on my bike. Beyond this, the route of The Ridgeway seemed to snap around a bit, particularly when it reached the A338 road. I then passed an Iron Age hill-fort called Segsbury Castle, but the long grass was too sodden with last night's rain for me to contemplate doing the customary circular walk.

The scenery mostly consisted of open, grassy fields and I eventually caught up with a male jogger and asked him how far it was to the nearest pub. He gave me directions to one about six miles ahead, and with this goal in sight, I continued, only for him to pass me again when I paused to read a sign (that old cat and mouse game again).

The trail seemed to undulate more after this and I climbed to pass the highest point in Oxfordshire – White Horse Hill, which tops out at 856 feet above sea level. There is another ancient hill-fort here in the form of Uffington Castle. Near to this is the Uffington White Horse which is a chalk carving dating from the late Bronze Age, the oldest white horse figure in Britain. In hindsight, I was something of a Philistine in not straying from the ancient roadway to view these historic earthworks, but I guess the lure of a pub and the push of the drizzly rain combined to keep me pedalling relentlessly.

A little further on was a stone burial chamber, known as Wayland's Smithy, a Neolithic long barrow. 'Barrow' in this instance refers to a tumulus, which is a mound of earth and stones raised over a grave; tumulus being Latin for 'mound.'

The original timber chambered oval barrow was probably built between 3,590 and 3,550BC, whilst the stone chambered long barrow that we see today was constructed between 3,460 and 3,400BC. Either way, I was about to witness something around five and a half thousand years old. To put this into perspective, it would be the best part of another millennium before the Great Pyramid at Giza was built or the first stones were raised at Stonehenge.

This time, I was sufficiently enticed to detour from my route. The barrow was reached via a narrow little path through high weeds that came off on the north side of The Ridgeway.

A couple were enjoying a picnic on top of the stone tomb, and after pleasantries, they agreed to take a photo of me beside the large stones at the entrance. I bravely handed over my phone to enable this. Interestingly, this barrow marked a transition from wooden to stone burial chambers. Wayland or Wolund was a Germanic smith-god and that the name was given to the site by Saxons who settled in the area many millennia later.

It was when I reached the next B-road that I knew I was nearing the pub. The rain was intensifying again, so I turned right and eventually began a steep descent off of the ridge to the village of Ashbury. The speedometer on my bike registered 32 miles per hour as I freewheeled down to this quaint little village of thatched cottages. A shroud of drizzle seemed to hang in the air, but this had no effect on the natural charm of the place. The pub was very picturesque too, and soon I was safely inside, ordering salmon and cream cheese on posh bread with a pot of tea. Delicious!

The local accents here were what I regard as 'proper West Country.' I had met some girls from Swindon (around six miles away) at a wedding some time before, and found their accents to be very different in a 'Where on earth are you from?' kind of way.

Upon leaving the pub I braced myself and cycled back up the hill to resume my westward course along The Ridgeway. I passed a transmitter beacon and then descended to a road to bridge the M4 and cross the wide, straight B4192 road, which streaked towards Swindon like an arrow. There were great views to the north, as ever. The grassy trail beyond climbed steeply back onto the hills. By now I was walking such inclines, too drained of energy to attempt to pedal.

Rain threatened again, and the path curved slowly southward, with the high weeds making sure that I could get the maximum saturation possible from the available wetness. I passed a rusty looking wagon and was tempted by the opportunity it provided for shelter.

Later, byway status was regained and the trail crossed a road and gradually curved back to resume a westward course, descending steeply through trees into the deep north-south valley of the River Og. I was just to the south of the village of Ogbourne St George, and by now the rain was carping on a bit, so upon reaching a reasonably main looking road, I turned right and headed northward into the village.

As it was still late afternoon, the pub was closed (how quaint), so I popped into a hotel and ordered a coffee, which I enjoyed in a quiet holding area just away from the main bar. I chatted to a man about the lack of a village shop there, which gave me a platform to proselytise about rural decline and the fact that successive governments have shown about as much concern over this issue as I have about the colour of Jeremy Clarkson's gear knob.

Those who are confused by this reference are reminded that the former presenter of the BBC's 'Top Gear' motoring programme once proclaimed, "I care more about the colour of the gear knob on my Mercedes SLK than the amount of carbon it produces." Whilst Clarkson always gets the reaction to his controversial one-liners that one would expect, I sometimes suspect that he is playing a character to a certain extent, and that maybe it is best to view his remarks that way and take our climate advice from the scientists.

Suitably reinvigorated, I returned along the road and turned right, back onto The Ridgeway, which began with another long climb, up out of the valley. This was a grassy trail now, passing another Iron Age earthwork – Barbury Castle. I circumnavigated this (as in some ancient Druidic ritual).

There followed another steep drop, followed by the inevitable climb, and the views back towards the hills beyond Ogbourne St George provided an impressive vista. The Ridgeway route was nearing its conclusion, like an old man slowly running out of steam. The long, slow descent southward to the valley of the River Kennet was heavy going, as the trail had become deeply rutted. The Kennet Valley was both ahead and to my right, as the river changes course ninety degrees near West Kennett (note two 'T's). It was about two miles shy of the end of the trail that I decided to abandon the route, for the byway was clearly no longer in an amenable mood for cyclists.

I headed off to the right, along what seemed like the roughest Sustrans cycle route I have ever encountered; Sustrans being the charity that maintains the National Cycle Network, which usually ensures a certain level of smoothness on its designated routes.

I headed for the village of Avebury, which is something of a Mecca for discerning tourists, being situated in the centre of a stone circle, which is reputedly the largest in the world, made up of a series of reasonably evenly spaced obelisks. The construction of this henge began around 2700BC, giving it a couple of hundred years head start on Stonehenge. The beauty is that you can walk around the stones freely, and I mean freely in both senses of the word. You see, it isn't necessary for every facet of our heritage to become a capitalist money-grab, so don't let anyone tell you otherwise!

The A4361 runs from north to south right through the village, and consequently through the stone circle, with a couple of sharp bends in its course. This is actually a cunningly renumbered section of the A361, which is a monster of a road running from Ilfracombe on the north coast of Devon, all the way to its junction with the A5 at Kilsby near the Northampton-Warwickshire border. It is the longest three-digit A-road in the UK. You don't care, do you?

Anyway, a four has been welded onto the number in the vicinity of Avebury, presumably to discourage through traffic, as there are certainly enough tourists milling around to create a bottleneck.

The Red Lion pub at the centre of the village was quaint and seemed to be a hive of activity. I enjoyed a steak with peppercorn sauce in a dining area down one side of the pub and then returned to the main bar, where I began to talk to an American woman who was there to soak up the history.

I decided to text a friend in the nearby boom-town of Swindon. Those of you with Columbo-like detection skills may have deduced that the wedding I attended where I'd first experienced the local accent was his. I wondered if I could persuade him to sojourn his marital bliss for a couple of hours and meet me for a catch up.

As he was travelling by car, he was unimpressed by the pub's 'pay and display' car park. No doubt Clarkson would have felt the same, and I must admit it does seem a little like cashing in on gullible tourists, although you could argue that it is providing them with a much needed parking space from which to explore the village.

Our chat was interesting, for at the time I was somewhat envious of his married life, as most of the dates I had been on were generally about as much fun as an intestinal biopsy - without anaesthetic! I remember taking one of my books to a pub in Maidstone in Kent to try to impress one such potential date. Leaving the table to visit the loo, I returned to find both the girl and the book gone. Now, nobody had ever gone to such desperate lengths to acquire one of my books before, but I wondered, would it have been worse if she'd left the book? Perhaps this was the most oblique form of underhanded compliment I'd ever experienced.

Other experiences included striking up a conversation with a girl from Cornwall who didn't seem to realise that 'Are you drunk?' is not a particularly good opening line to speak to a 'stone cold sober' potential partner. Another prospective date suggested a visit to The Holocaust Exhibition in the Imperial War Museum. Interesting though it was, it was hardly a place to elicit romantic vibes.

As you can see, I was pretty disillusioned with all of it and vowed to be a 'metal machine man' with no romantic ambitions. For a visual image of this, look at Lou Reed's pose on the album cover of 'Metal Machine Music,' a delightfully unlistenable cacophony from 1977.

My friend related all this to his own experiences which had led him to marry a girl from Swindon who he'd met on holiday, but at the time I was rather cynical. Exactly one year later I would meet future wife, so if this book achieves anything perhaps it is just a little bit of hope for the disenfranchised.

Eventually a largish man piped up from a table next to us. He gave us an impromptu history lesson, elevating our conversation from the banal mechanics of dating to the lofty ways of Druidry. He informed us that all roads called 'The Ridgeway' ultimately lead to Avebury, each forming part of a network with this stone circle in Wiltshire as the Mecca of its day. I'm not sure how true this was, but it was interesting and added some mystery to our hitherto pragmatic discussions.

After learning more than we'd ever imagined there was to know about ley lines, it was time to leave. I was offered a bed in a warm, comfortable house in Swindon, but I stoically stuck to the hymn sheet of sleeping rough, opting to ride about four dusky miles northward along the A4361 before turning right to climb back

141

up onto the hills and rejoin The Ridgeway, with the possibility of laying on a ley line for the night. It was dark by now, so this was something of a sightless sprint on the bike.

The Ridgeway had been punctuated with large copses from the moment I'd pedalled up onto the hills beyond Goring, so I knew exactly where I could set up camp - a small, circular woodland overlooking the valley below. I struggled a little to set up my tarpaulin as the wind whistled through the trees. This relentless rustling would mean that my sleep would be broken, in spite of this being a pretty good spot to camp.

I dreamed about walking in my home village, with my pace slowing until I was literally crawling on the ground and wondering why the simple act of walking had become impossible. I decided to sleep in a hedge and was concerned that I had the disorder known as chronic fatigue syndrome.

Was is a metaphor for tiring of the kind of dates I'd described to my friend, just a representation of my pace slowing on the bike during the previous day, or the Druidic vibes finally getting to me? Perhaps it was all three.

25) Superlative Silbury

I awoke early, and before long I was cruising back down the hill into the valley, which was when the rain started. I began to head south along the main road towards Avebury again, but ended up diving into a bus shelter and waiting for the downpour to pass.

After a while, I decided to make a dash for the village. I chained up my bike at the northern entrance to Avebury and began to walk the stone circle in an anti-clockwise fashion. However, the wet stuff began to pour again, so I promptly dived into the doorway of the church for shelter. It seemed almost incongruent to find a church in a place of such Druidic significance, so I took a wander inside to read the history of the place.

When I emerged again my spirits rose, for I was pleased to find a species of the lesser-spotted 'open' village shop. I purchased some comestibles and consumed them as I walked the remaining three quarters of the stone circle. There is a grass mound that runs around the outside of the circle and it was this that I was mostly walking.

Reunited with my bike, I then pedalled right through the village and out to the south, branching off onto a B-road, which was more like a lane, down to the A4 - the rambling London to Bristol road. I turned right to check out Silbury Hill from either side. This is the largest man-made mound in Europe, being around 130 feet in height, and was probably built between around 2470BC and 2350BC.

The intended use of the mound is unknown, but I quite like the legend that the devil was carrying a shovel of soil which he planned to dump on nearby Marlborough. The myth states that he was either outwitted by a cobbler or apprehended by some priests and consequently dumped it there.

More seriously, it is believed that the mound is linked to the other prehistoric sites in the area, such as the West Kennet Long Barrow (on the nearby hills and with one 'T' like the river) and Avebury Henge which I'd wandered around earlier. The elite few would use these sites to elevate themselves above the masses. I mused that nothing much has changed, for this seems similar to the way that modern office blocks are used today. Note how the chief executive of the company will always be on the uppermost floor and how these buildings get taller and taller every year in order not to be outdone by a rival 'god.'

I recently read a book by the German philosopher Nietzsche. He postulated many things about Christianity that are a challenge to anybody who has been brought up with such a background, but I find it particularly hard to agree with his suggestion that some people should naturally be elevated to an aristocratic class. To quote, he says, "No one any longer possesses today the courage to claim special privileges or the right to rule... the aristocratic outlook has been undermined most deeply by the lie of equality of souls."

Whilst concurring that we shouldn't be dominated by religious leaders (in the way that things would have in Silbury's heyday), I still think the 'equality of souls' as he calls it has been a levelling measure in society, and that the wider the division between rich and poor, elite and proletariat, the worse society is in almost every aspect - a basic psychological fact that modern day elitists loathe to admit.

I expected to find a path leading to the top of the mound so I could feel like an ancient revered figure, but I found my access to be prevented, so it was back to the A4 for a little ride westward towards the roundabout with the A4361 and A361, which as you know are really one and the same. I was uncertain what to do next, for I was feeling increasingly tired (like in last night's dream) and the weather was showing no sign of improvement. Logically, I did what any sensible person would do and headed for the pub.

I enjoyed a pint of Wadsworth's bitter in the large, roadside inn which had the look of a hotel. Rain hung like a shroud over the hills to the south, so I soon dismissed the idea of riding up over them against a head-wind towards Salisbury. Draining my glass, I sent myself scuttling back to Avebury again. Perhaps there was something mysterious about the way this place kept luring me back inside its stone circle from every conceivable direction. However, this time, I rode straight through and out the other side towards Swindon.

The floor of the valley seemed to rise as I headed northward towards the source of the River Kennet. The road made a long, steady climb to the summit, where I briefly sheltered beneath a large bush at a junction with a little lane. I prepared myself up for my final approach to Swindon, like a pilot coming in to land.

Nearby is the small town of Royal Wootton Bassett, one of only three places in the UK with the prefix 'Royal,' the other two being Tunbridge Wells and Leamington Spa. The town had become known for its informal military repatriation funeral processions, where the coffins of British servicemen and women passed through the town en route from RAF Lyneham to the John Radcliffe Hospital in Oxford. The streets were lined with reverent people to commemorate each loss, in spite of the unpopularity of the wars in Afghanistan and Iraq. The 'Royal' prefix was bestowed upon the town in 2011.

The long descent into Swindon was a breeze, bridging the M4 and pressing on through myriad suburbs. The sun came out, and by the time I reached the centre I was hot, especially after a surprise hill to climb.

Much as temptation should have compelled me to explore this old railway town that has transformed itself into a business hub, in the way that my hometown of Ashford in Kent is attempting to do (but not quite achieving), fatigue had got the better of me, and the sight of the railway station was like the proverbial pool of water in the desert.

I was soon relaxing on a train heading for London's Paddington station. As it expediently zipped its way towards Reading, I gazed south at the ridge of hills that I'd cycled along during the last few days. I was surprised at how much ground I had traversed in that short space of time.

For now, I just had that death-defying sprint across London to St Pancras to undertake, and it is London that we explore next, for my preceding trip, just a month before, had been to cycle the Thames Path from the centre of the capital to Reading. So get your jellied eels and your Chas and Dave records at the ready. 'Gor blimey guv'nor, we're going dahn The Thames!'

THAMES PATH

26) Runnymede's Revenge

The Thames is the UK's second longest river, running for 215 miles from deepest Gloucestershire to emerge into the North Sea between Essex and Kent, thus giving the name to an entire dialect known as 'estuary English.'

The most famous section is of course via London. The first bridge encountered when travelling upriver is the Queen Elizabeth II Bridge between Dartford and Thurrock, often mistitled as the M25 – this little section is actually numbered A282. The M25 is not a complete circle. In fact all of London's ring roads are a bit of a bodge.

The North Circular and South Circular are linked by the Woolwich Ferry, and whilst the North Circular makes a noble attempt at being half of a proper ring road, you get the impression that the South Circular really can't be bothered and would prefer to be down the pub. Then there's the inner ring road, which is basically just a collection of streets which seemed to have got drunk one night and signed some kind of ring road agreement not knowing what it was.

When you look at the Garden Ring (inner), Third Ring (middle) and Moscow Ring (outer) in Russia's capital city, there is really no comparison. No wonder some folk refer to President Putin as 'The Lord of the Rings.'

Anyway, travelling west from the QEII Bridge, the next crossing we encounter is Tower Bridge, perhaps the most easily recognisable bridge in the UK. Next up is London Bridge, which is the oldest of the city's crossings, established in 50AD and rebuilt many times, the last three of which were 1209, 1831 and 1973. It is of course the eponymous subject of the children's nursery rhyme 'London Bridge is falling down,' and it was the only bridge across The Thames in London until 1750 when Westminster Bridge first appeared.

A public footpath runs for the entire length of the river, and much of the eastern half can be cycled. I had ridden the section from Erith into Central London several years before as a day trip, but my proper Thames adventure took place during a fairly unsettled period in June, commencing at Charing Cross.

This was a fitting start because Charing Cross is the point from which all distances to London on UK road signs are

146

measured. The reason for this, according to the BBC website, was that the wife of King Edward I died while at a manor house in Lincoln and her body was taken to Westminster Abbey for a state burial. The King decided that twelve memorial crosses should be placed at each stopping point of the funeral procession and the final one was at Charing Cross. The original cross was south of the statue of King Edward I in Trafalgar Square and there is a plaque on the ground behind the statue stating that this is still the point from which all mileages are taken.

As I rode down the embankment from the station, myriad cathedral bells were ringing their midday chimes, and Big Ben (which is a bell not a clock tower) was no doubt heard among the din.

I soon picked up the Victoria Embankment road. This tamed dual carriageway by the river forms the end of a fairly interesting drive into London from the east, which tunnels beneath the docklands and Canary Wharf (the location of the UK's second highest building). It then runs through the city and under a short tunnel beneath the buildings before following The Thames from Tower Bridge to the Houses of Parliament. Mental note: I must video this journey sometime and post it on YouTube.

Interestingly, the word 'parliament' is taken from the old French word 'parlement,' meaning a discussion, derived from the verb 'parler' - to speak. I'd previously heard that the 'ment' part originates from the French verb 'mentir' – to lie. Although I prefer this definition as it suits my view of most politicians, I'm afraid I cannot corroborate it.

From here I must have continued past Westminster Abbey and along Millbank (note the hazy memory), at some point deciding to switch to the south bank, as I had found nothing resembling a signed cycle route so far. Deduction tells me that I would have then cycled through Battersea Park.

Now, no music fan could pass through this area without mentioning the imposing structure of Battersea Power Station, which famously features in Pink Floyd's 1977 cover for the album 'Animals,' complete with inflatable pig. After Abbey Road, this must surely be the discerning music lover's second most important stop in London. In my opinion third would be Berwick Street, as featured on the Oasis album '(What's the Story) Morning Glory?' but perhaps I'm getting into debatable territory now.

Annoyingly, it seemed as though the Thames Path was allergic to The Thames, for as soon as I found a defined footpath as such, it seemed to deviate off around various offices. I eventually found a small convenience store in a square and emerged triumphantly with a pasty and a drink. As I consumed these, the wet stuff began to fall out of the sky and I found myself sheltering beneath an awning. I had visions of having to abandon this ride and return home within a matter of hours.

Once the shower had passed, I decided to cross the river via Putney Bridge, deciding that perhaps the north bank was going to provide me with a more consistent pathway after all. I was changing sides more often than a premiership football player.

I headed into a park by All Saints Church and it was at this point that the rain upped the ante, forcing me to seek immediate shelter. Once again, the shower passed, and as soon as it did, the other cyclists and walkers sheltering all sprang back into action silently. It was like watching meerkats in a nature film, or as if somebody had briefly pressed the pause button on the TV remote.

The path made a deviation around Fulham Stadium, and before long I'd had enough of the north bank again, and decided to cross via Barnes Bridge – this consisting of a footbridge next to a rail bridge. There was a formidable flight of steps to haul my bike down on the opposite side.

It wasn't long before the path had finally whipped itself up into a proper trail. At last! Soon I was flying past Kew Gardens, and the river had a much greener feel to it than the famous city section dominated by shards and gherkins. As I rounded the curve towards Richmond Bridge, the scene before me looked positively quaint.

This section of the path was bustling with shops and stalls, feeling similar to those sections of sea-wall where there are ice cream stands and deck chairs. As expected, signs instructed me to dismount.

The stone bridge at Richmond upon Thames is the oldest remaining Thames bridge in London, dating from 1777. The pleasant vibes seduced me into making a pit stop, and I headed for the café beneath the bridge for a life-affirming cup of tea.

Beyond Richmond, the river curves beside a large, green area known as Petersham Meadow. Overlooking this is the ridge upon which Richmond Park stands, where deer roam freely in the heathland. At this point one barely gets the feel of being in a big city at all. This section of path regularly floods when the river is high, and I continued past Ham Meadow.

This bucolic feeling was short-lived though, as I soon found myself coming back into suburbia. The riverbank at Kingston upon Thames has a well-to-do air about it and I sped through this, eager to be returned to a more rural scene. Curiously, Kingston upon

Thames is the administrative centre of Surrey, in spite of being within the boundaries of Greater London. In fact, even Richmond upon Thames was part of the provincial county until 1965

I didn't realise that the Thames Path switches to the north bank here. Exiled to the road, I consequently found myself being channelled further and further south, away from the river. This is partly because the River Mole joins here, having flowed northward from the Surrey town of Dorking. The Thames seems to split into various channels and locks around here. I decided to ask a couple walking by for directions and eventually found my way to Hampton Court Bridge, the final bridge in Greater London, with the north bank in the metropolitan county and the south bank in Surrey.

This little deviation had robbed me of the chance of a view of Hampton Court Palace on the north bank. However, unknowingly I may have passed the 'boat cum recording studio' owned by Pink Floyd legend Dave Gilmour, which I understand is moored somewhere in the vicinity of Hurst Park. Personally I would have liked to have popped aboard for a cup of tea and chat with the guitar hero, but my schedule was tight. Another time perhaps!

Still on the south side, the next deviation was at Weybridge. Here, unsurprisingly, The Thames is joined by the River Wey. If you cast your mind back to the very beginning of this book, it is from the Wey Navigation that the Basingstoke Canal commences its course. There was a steep bridge over a lock, and then my route briefly ran southward by a tributary before reaching a road. Here I encountered my first hill of the day, with a climb towards Chertsey.

Signage was pretty good however, for this was now part of National Cycle Route 4. There was a pathway section across a meadow and the police had cordoned off the path at this point. I wondered if there had been a murder or something of that ilk as I negotiated my way around this with ease.

I was soon crossing The Thames via Chertsey Bridge. The river was now much narrower than the famed Central London section and the bridge was a similar quaint looking affair to the one at Richmond.

My route continued along a lane on the north side of the river at this point. This had creatively been named 'Thames Side'. I passed beneath the M3 bridge, carrying myriad vehicles from the city to Basingstoke, Winchester and Southampton, and my route soon reneged to 'track' status.

My next stop was in Staines, the town famous for Sacha Baron Cohen's character Ali G. The image this had given me of the town was way off the mark however, for as I neared the centre I found the riverbank to be very pleasant. I passed beneath the railway bridge and the area had an air of salubriousness about it, but not in the modern way which I'd felt at Kingston, which had instantly brought to mind young, smartly dressed professionals who fake their accents to aid their trajectory towards the top.

It was surely time for a beer. Well, sort of – I went in a large, airy bar beside the river and ordered a shandy with some fish and chips. As is the tradition, out came the diary and pen, in order to scrawl down a few notes about my adventure. I recall the barman becoming quite chatty upon catching a glimpse of my backpack. I returned to my seat to quaff a Guinness as my second drink.

The skies were beginning to look grey, and at this stage I was a little uncertain about this camping lark, having only undertaken two of these trips before.

Writing this book is beginning to make me feel like the scientists staring deeper and deeper into space, knowing that they are viewing older and older events and getting closer to the 'Big Bang' that started it all. In these early days, such trips were a far more ramshackle affair, for I wasn't even in possession of a groundsheet – the 'camp' was literally a sleeping bag flung on the deck. Thus the notion of finding some accommodation flashed into my mind, and as I left the pub I decided to do a search.

The first hotel (which I believe was on the opposite bank) was charging £100 for the night. Narrowly escaping a cardiac arrest, I was sent reeling in the direction of Travelodge, where a sign outside promised rooms from £19. I ventured in and asked if any of these £19 rooms were available and was duly informed that they had to be booked online. At the time smartphones weren't so widely popular, 'tablets' were something you took for a headache and I'd forgotten to pack my desktop computer and monitor.

After riding to a garage for some water, I took a phone call while I wandered down by the arched bridge across the river. It felt as though I was providing a telephone counselling service.

After a good twenty minutes of that, I crossed to the south bank and toyed with the idea of camping beneath one of the secluded arches, surrounded by bushes, but I already had images of drunks coming down there after kick-out to 'drain the main vein' as some people call it. The idea of a shower in uric acid definitely wasn't on my tick-list. So I pressed on.

The Thames splits into a lot of locks and channels at this point, and I felt a sense of achievement, for the river was now a decidedly different beast to the one I'd began my ride along earlier in Central London.

Passing beneath the M25, I now felt that I was truly out of the metropolis, and I made a mental note of the fact that should heavy rain ensue in the night, I could always hammer it back to this point and shelter beneath the roaring traffic.

Beyond this I came to Runnymede, famed for being the place where King John agreed to seal the Magna Carta on June 15th 1215, an event occasionally cited as the birthplace of modern democracy. There is a memorial to John F. Kennedy too, which I understand is situated upon land that was actually given to the USA as a gift. I've no idea how they're going to take their gift home but as my grandmother once said, 'Anything is possible in this enlightened age!'

I passed over a section of open grassland between the river and the A308 which was running to my left. Beyond the road, to the south, I could see wooded hills. This was my first glimpse of an actual escarpment close to The Thames. There was a 'parkland' feel to the area, with the river hidden behind spindly bushes on my right. I carried on to the village of Old Windsor, where the path became sandwiched between expensive looking properties and the water, but I eventually deduced that my best option for finding a secluded camping area was back at Runnymede, behind those bushes.

I was soon cocooned within my sleeping bag. A hot night ensued, but thankfully rain didn't come. Instead I was visited by an insect of some kind and bitten heartily on the top lip, awaking to find it feeling as though it had been pumped full of anaesthetic. Either way, it was the lesser of two evils when I thought back to the prospect of waking up surrounded by Ali G and chums beneath that bridge in Staines.

27) Henley Heart Attack

I rose at 9.45am and was soon on the trail once more, riding merrily with a bemused feeling as to what could have bitten me. I had dark images of an adder lashing its tongue at me in the night while I was blissfully unaware. It had been a pretty good night's sleep all things considering, and the sound of people walking along the path nearby in the early morning sun had only broken my slumber for the briefest of moments.

As I wound into action, the first mile or two was familiar from last night's search for a spot to camp, but beyond Old Windsor I found myself diverted away from the river and onto a B-road via the village of Datchet.

I was soon approaching Windsor, with its castle dominating the skyline as I rode in triumphantly, passing green recreational land. The town was originally called New Windsor to distinguish itself from the village I'd cycled through earlier. William the Conqueror established a castle here at around 1070. The castle was developed and expanded, most notably under Edward III in the 1360s. Ten British monarchs are buried in the chapel here, including Henry VI who was possibly murdered and thus attracted many pilgrims to the site.

The history doesn't end with the castle though. Windsor's bridge over The Thames was the earliest between Staines and Reading, dating back to the twelfth century, although remarkable evidence of a Bronze Age bridge dating from around 1400BC-1300BC has been found. Another little known fact is that from 1883 to 1885, the London Underground's District Line services ran as far as Windsor too.

Call me a Philistine, but in spite of the town being steeped in history and tourist interest, I had just one thing on my mind – a fry-up!

I found a café and availed myself of a 'half breakfast' which was ample for me. The town centre seemed fairly quiet as I sat staring out of the window over a cup of tea, like the old man in Ralph McTell's 'Streets of London' song.

Once back on the trail beside the river, the air of ludicrous wealth was all-pervading. I rode past homes that could easily be described as mansions. At one point there was a wooden footbridge over The Thames and I crossed it in accordance with the signs for cyclists. However, the designated route deviated away from the river, defeating the object of a Thames ride for me, so I crossed back and continued on the footpath - a little bit naughty I know.

I remember the river being lined with trees at this point, with lakes nearby on the north side. There is also a little spur of The Thames called the Jubilee River to the north, which parts company just east of Windsor and rejoins just north of Maidenhead.

Soon I was passing beneath the London to South Wales motorway (M4) and without knowing it, I'd also passed the village of Bray, home of two of the four three-Michelin-starred restaurants in the UK. One of these is called The Fat Duck and is owned by famed TV chef Heston Blumenthal. It topped a list of the fifty best restaurants in the world in 2005. The other restaurant, called The Waterside Inn, is the only restaurant in the UK to retain three Michelin stars for 25 years, achieving this feat in 2010. Suddenly, my Windsor half breakfast seems light years away, and in hindsight I wish I'd known about the village at the time and had a nose at the place.

Furthermore, esteemed TV presenter Michael Parkinson lives within the village. I imagine that the village has rather less pride in the fact that it was also home to disgraced TV star Rolf Harris. Ugh!

The river curved northward at roughly this point, and the next town I reached was Maidenhead, which straddles the section of single carriageway A4 between London and Reading.

As I entered the town I passed beneath the 1838 Brunel-built railway bridge. This part of the town seemed very pleasant and I crossed the road bridge to frequent a little shop, purchasing some Lucozade and consuming it nearby. The wall of tiredness was beginning to hit me, so I hoped flooding my system with glucose might wake me up a bit.

I then continued beside the river, northward along the west bank, noticing the wooded hill on the opposite side. I began to get that feeling of The Thames doing a low-key impression of the gorge sections of the Rhine, but really this was all in my Lucozade-infused mind.

There were certain points where the ultra-rich have commandeered the riverside for their own exclusive properties, and the proles on the path have to deviate. One of these diversions was via the village of Cookham, the name perhaps echoing the sentiment of those wealthy riverside dwellers towards the plebs.

Following the signs, I was eventually returned to the riverside, but the path was becoming much less suitable for cycling, with the odd obstruction thrown in for good measure. The riverside trail was now grassy and the scenery quite open.

I came to a railway bridge with a foot crossing, this being the single-track branch line from Maidenhead to Marlow. Confused as to which side would be the best for me to continue my illegal ride, I asked some hikers. Their info proved invaluable, and I crossed to the village of Bourne End, which was clearly a boat orientated place. Now on the east bank again, I briefly relished the smoothness of tarmac beneath my wheels, but soon found myself pounding the grass again as the river rounded another bend and I resumed a westward course.

There was a small line of dirt worn into the grass, and my pace seemed quite speedy as I zipped along it, with the rail line running parallel to my right and open fields all around me. There were plenty of swing gates bunged in to deter errant cyclists like myself, but I had no intention of throwing in the towel and resorting to roads. I don't really understand why this section is not officially available for cyclists; the grassy strip beside the river is wide, so collision is unlikely, but then the same could be said of much of the Royal Military Canal in Kent, and I'm sure you recall the red-faced, spleen rupturing rage inflicted upon me there.

The next place I encountered was Marlow, where the path was sandwiched between brick walls as I neared the centre. There is an interesting suspension bridge over the river at the southern end of the main street. This was built in 1832. I also noticed that it has won numerous 'best kept village' competitions in spite of being what I would describe as a small country town. T.S. Elliot lived in the town's West Street during the World War I.

I quickly located a pub and prepared myself for a wallet emptying experience as I bravely ordered a pint of Guinness, perhaps for its hearty iron content as much as anything. I was pleasantly surprised to find the price to be just £3.10, proving that being in County Bucks needn't cost mega-bucks. (A pint of the black stuff was around £3.50 in Kent at the time of my visit.)

I had a virtual drink with my 'phone a friend' friend, which basically means me supping a pint while we exchange text messages. So often I find myself texting absent friends on a lone visit to the pub. Whether or not technology is bringing people together or forcing them apart is a debate where your opinion will largely depend on which side of forty you are.

I am typing this as I approach the age at which life begins, and as pub after pub closes forever, I find myself gradually moving towards the Philistine camp, in spite of holding together several friendships on a predominantly technology-dependent basis. Yet you could argue that technology is the string from which friendships often hang - friendships that may have been all but lost due to logistics in the pre-mobile-phone era.

I decided to take a ride over the suspension bridge and back again, before continuing along the north bank via a fun fair which was taking place on a green near the river.

After a few miles, the path swapped back to the south side courtesy of another footbridge. Are you getting dizzy visualising all these swaps yet? Beyond this, the route remained very much in 'grassy meadows' mode, although at one point the path veered away up a hillside through farmland, before finding its way back to the river, helped by gravity.

Then another long, sweeping bend meant another change in direction and I would find myself heading south as I neared the town of Henley-on-Thames. Henley Church could be seen on the opposite side as the bend ensued, and it was at this point that the clouds, which had been steadily increasing all day, finally crossed that line from white to grey. The wind had been increasing too, but luckily, it was now behind me. The path regained a surface for the last mile or two and I was positively speeding along.

The town is of course famous for its regatta, and I passed myriad boats as I cruised past greens where I could imagine smartly dressed folk drinking Pimms. Upon reaching the centre of Henley, I crossed the bridge and swiftly located a snug, hotel bar. I opted for a pint of Henley Gold, which was a light coloured ale, described in my diary, perhaps incorrectly, as a cross between bitter and lager. It seems hard to imagine but this may have been the first time I encountered a pint of 'gold bitter.'

These beers have only been around for a nanosecond in terms of brewing history, and Hop Back Brewery's Summer Lightning is often claimed to have been the first to be brewed all year round, appearing in the late eighties. Sometimes referred to as a 'summer ale,' these light coloured brews have become increasingly popular with those who associate the darker ales with 'a pint of heavy.' It's all in the mind I'm sure.

I ordered a salmon sandwich, and sat in a quiet area away from the bar. However, when I wandered a little to get a better feel of the place I nearly had an embolism. The price list for the rooms was as follows:

Single room - £300
Double room - £500
Deluxe room - £600

Now, don't get me wrong. The ambience was very nice and Henley is an affluent town as we well know, but really? For that money I'd expect to see crystal chandeliers hanging from every ceiling and gold plated handrails leading upstairs to the rooms. Like much of the stuff that the elite lap up, I tend this think it's all a bit 'emperor's new clothes.' I'm all for trying out new places, but if it's going to cost me a week's wages for one night at a hotel I'm afraid I'll stick with Travelodge. That's if I can cram the computer into my rucksack to book it of course.

With the skies looking angry now, I had dismissed the idea of camping out and was eager to find somewhere to stay, more along the lines of 'chez doss house.' I couldn't see myself finding anywhere suitable in Henley, and after a phone call to another friend, no doubt containing a venting about our beloved politicians, I pressed on towards Berkshire's county town – Reading.

The riverside path (now on the west bank again) passed over a series of long, wooden bridges as I headed south out of Henley. I passed a garden with a railway track running around it, and as I left the town, the scenery was that of meadows, with insects flying in and out of the long reeds and bushes. At the time this foliage was so high that I couldn't even see The Thames over the top of it, and the way these reeds were encroaching on the path gave me a sensation that it could be prone to flooding.

The trail switched to the east bank at Sonning Bridge, and once a hard surface had returned and the grass had tamed itself into mowed parkland, I knew I was approaching Reading. Grey, square industrial buildings began to invade my field of vision too.

The Thames re-establishes a longitudinal route at this point and I branched off of the westward-bound towpath at the junction with the Kennet and Avon Canal, riding into the town beside terraces and passing a suburban pub, if my memory serves me well.

This was my first experience of Reading town centre (and not to be my last, as you will recall). The grey skies propelled me in the direction of the nearest hotel. Now, bearing in mind that at the time I had a strict policy of never paying over £30 for a room, you'll understand how the £79 price for a single room propelled me back out again as quickly as a boot up the posterior. As I write this looking back a few years, such a policy seems rather miserly, for the £30 room has since joined the four-leaf clover and the snake's foot in obscurity.

Reluctantly I decided to call an end to this particular trip. It was time for a few hours of clickety-clack back to the green and pleasant county of Kent via the capital city.

I was stunned at how as late as 10.50pm besuited commuters were still alighting the trains from London, knowing that they'd be yo-yoing back to the city again in a mere seven hours time. These must be people who truly live their jobs, with total dedication to the ethic of work. Personally I'd rather go for less money and a home-life, but it's horses for courses I guess - in their case workhorses!

The rain began when I reached the Kentish town of Ashford, and having missed the last train to my village, I ditched the option of cycling in favour of a taxi. I would wake up the next morning to a positive deluge. I had made the right decision.

SOMERSET

28) Suspense in Bristol

Climbing back into our DeLorean and winding it up to 88 miles per hour, we emerge almost a year earlier. It is now July and I am about to embark on a trip where I aimed to tick off a few gems from my 'must see in England' list.

However, the trip almost didn't happen, for as I went to pump up one of my bike tyres I somehow managed to rip the valve clean off. I wandered along to the local bike shop which was closed, but luckily the owner's wife came down from the flat above especially and opened it so I could purchase a new inner tube.

The next challenge was fitting it. Amazingly I had cycled avidly since the age of about nine (so 25 years at this point) but had never performed even the most basic mechanical task on the bike other than fixing the odd puncture. In the early days I would use the bicycle repair man known as 'Dad,' and in later years when I found myself living just 300 yards from a bike shop, I'd just wheel it along and announce, "Another fine mess for you to sort out!"

Removing the wheel and changing the tube was remarkably easy. The only problem was that I found myself unable to pump up this new tube. I didn't have the heart to drag 'Mrs bike shop' out of her house again, so this time I wheeled my velocipede down to the village garage and a local mechanic saved the day.

This 'village' service was one of the things I'd miss during my later spell living in the seaside town of Folkestone. There is much that is questionable about rural life, such as the endless gossip, the neurotic fear of change, the slow erosion of services and the sheer spite that is unearthed if your dare to challenge the status quo, but in my opinion personal service of this kind, pubs where you're never a stranger and friendly 'good mornings' still give country life the edge.

I wolfed down a quick sardine sandwich, purchased my ticket at the station and finally broke free of the gravitational pull of the village as the train thundered up the hill towards Ashford. At this point I knew nothing about the arcane ways in which you can reduce a train fare using railcards and your degree in rail network knowledge; I simply paid through the nose without question.

Boarding the same train as me was a young lady who claimed to be a backing singer with a tribute band known as The

Australian Pink Floyd. I wonder how long it took to come up with that for a name.

I think she was on her way to Birmingham on this particular day, and I was informed that her ex was on the verge of becoming famous too. I was amazed to find people making a career out of music living in my own village, previously assuming that you had to be based in London to get anywhere with something creative.

I changed trains at Ashford and again at Waterloo. On the Salisbury train I was asked to move my bike to the designated biking carriage. I find that guards operate a imprecise policy on this. Some are quite happy for you to jump on the nearest carriage and put the bike across the doors on the non-platform side, while others have an almost Gestapo-like intolerance for two-wheeled contraptions. Soon after this the air conditioning packed up, and then we got stuck behind a freight train. You've got to love British train travel!

The final train to Bath was very scenic as we emerged into the valley of The Avon just before Bradford. When I finally alighted, I was itching to get cycling, but as this was my first visit to Bath I was in need of a map and promptly made my way to a branch of WH Smith.

It seems crazy now, but such was my haste to get mobile, that I eschewed all the delights of Bath and just headed for the river path, following this until it terminated at a road lined with industrial buildings. A little further, I finally found the beginning of the thirteen-mile-long former rail route to Bristol – I could relax now, for this trail was the first 'box' on my West Country tick-list.

Maybe my intention was to ride a big loop over the next few days and explore Bath properly at the end, or maybe, as this was only the second of these cycling trips I'd undertaken, my focus was too much on the fitness part to bother with such cerebral activities as tourism.

The Bath and Bristol Railway Path is a piece of history, being the first cycleway opened by the cycling charity Sustrans who converted it between 1979 and 1986. The path made a long, slow curve to the right around a steep, wooded hill, and after a while I was heading northward rather than west, running alongside the single-track Avon Valley Railway, a three-mile-long heritage line offering steam train rides from Avon Riverside via Bitton and Oldland. The views behind and to the east were of impressive rolling hills. However, the bucolic scene was interrupted by the fact that somebody had decided to daub the place with slogans along the lines of, 'Bikes are good. Trains pollute.'

Much as I admire the green sentiment, I hardly think a small, steam line in the West Country is the world's biggest concern when it comes to climate change. If the sloganeer never uses electricity or any other form of transport apart from his or her bike, then I am impressed, but if not I'd like to offer the following slogan, 'Trains pollute. Cars, vans, lorries, buses, planes, helicopters, rockets, amphibious landing craft, etc. pollute more!'

I passed a yard with some steam engines in, and after some more parallel running with the steam line, the rails ended and I spotted another slogan stating, 'Nicer here. No rails, no fences!' Maybe I should have daubed one a little further saying, 'Nicer still here. No graffiti!'

After a while, I encountered an area where the A4174 ring road has made a right hash of the route, diverting it from the trackbed. There was formerly a rail junction here, where the line I had ridden from Bath met the former Bristol to Gloucester line. Both the routes were operated by Midland Railway and are now redundant. The only route between Bristol and Bath today is the shorter Great Western route which runs to the south of the River Avon, Meanwhile, the main route from Bath to Gloucester now heads north from the city centre towards Filton, bears east towards London and then north again near Yate, where the former Bristol to Gloucester route remains.

So at this point, my ride turned left, and after passing a stately looking ruined station to my right, it felt like I was riding on the cycleway equivalent of a motorway, with a continuous stream of bikes coming out of Bristol and numbered exits to various roads. Presumably the riders were coming home from work.

The route pummels its way through a reasonably long tunnel beneath Staple Hill. It was nice and cool and reasonably well-lit for its entire length. I relished this experience, as usually these cycleway conversion paths are routed up over the top when encountering tunnels. It was a long, straight, slowly descending tunnel, and you could see the light at the end all the way through. For me, it was quite a surreal experience to be honest, but I imagine that this feeling fades if you bike through it every day to work.

The only time I'd ridden through an old railway tunnel before was in Heathfield, East Sussex, where there is a tunnel beneath the ridge of hills at the end of the Cuckoo Trail. I recall cycling through the gently curving tunnel some time before it was briefly opened to the public officially, receiving bemused looks from a courting couple who were canoodling on a bench near the entrance, expecting to be undisturbed near the mouth of a boarded up railway tunnel. I think a cyclist casually pedalling out of the black hole was the last thing they envisaged.

Anyway, back to Bristol, and my descent continued beneath modern road bridges and past parkland to the city centre. I eventually found my way to the river and was lured by The Riverside Inn, a small establishment at the side of the road. Upon entering, I was pleased to see a huge collection of vinyl records on a shelf. This was clearly an urban pub aimed at music lovers. The tattooed barmaid was very pleasant to talk to and after imbibing the contents of a pint glass, it was time to move on.

The riverside ride through the centre of Bristol was very pleasant in the early evening sunshine. The Avon was lined with fashionable outdoor cafés and had an air of youthful affluence about it – that feeling you always get in university towns.

I rode around an inlet where the River Frome joins The Avon, and as I came out of the city centre I remember struggling to stay by the river, as industrial buildings began to encroach. I ended up at a busy gyratory system and started off riding beside the north bank of The Avon along the A4, but as I neared Clifton Suspension Bridge, I realised that the cycle route was now on the opposite bank. Why don't they sign these things consistently?

So it was back to the gyratory system and over the river on Brunel Way – now there's a clue for you if ever there was one. I then picked up the cycle path, and before long I was in a deep gorge, passing beneath the aforementioned bridge, which carries a B-road across at a height of just under 250 feet above the high water level.

It was built to a design by Isambard Kingdom Brunel although he never saw its completion, shuffling off this mortal coil in 1859. The bridge finally opened in 1864. Traditionally the bridge linked Gloucestershire on the north side with Somerset on the south side. These counties have since been chopped about so many times that it makes your head spin.

There was a railway line to the left of the trail as I rode, and every now and then there would be wooded areas that I registered as possible places to camp. The deep, rocky gorge, gradually became less dramatic as I continued, eventually levelling out into open farmland. The grass always seems a much deeper and more satisfying green in these south-western counties to me. Could it be due to extra rainfall than our parched lawns get in The South-East?

The trail eventually brought me out to a track which climbed to a little village called Ham Green. I am not sure where Ham

Green ends and Pill starts, but I found them to be a lively looking combined community with a striking rail viaduct across the middle.

It seems that gentrification had yet to reach this locale at the time, for I went into a pub hoping for a slap up meal, only to find that food wasn't served. I mused that back in Kent a village pub simply cannot survive on wet sales alone. Thus, I was directed to the next village, Easton-in-Gordano.

Now, my hopes were raised, for I was already familiar with this village's name thanks to the legendary West Country folk combo of Adge Cutler and the Wurzels: "In sunshine or in rain-o, Easton-in-Gordano, is the place for I to be!" This surely meant another tick on the West Country hit list.

Pill seamlessly merged again into Easton, and I wandered into a pub called The Kings Arms, not realising that I was on musical holy ground akin to Strawberry Fields or Penny Lane, for Adge name-checks this pub in the aforementioned song. I ordered a ploughman's supper (what else?) and a friendly local chatted while I ordered a drink.

As I ate at a table nearer the front of the pub, I remember somebody else exchanging a few words as he passed. I told him that I was from Kent and that I was exploring the area by bike. It was a bit like being a rock star for a day, for everybody I met seemed genuinely interested in what I was doing. Not in a Kentish, 'That's nice, now I must go and count my money' kind of way, but in a genuine Wurzelish (or even 'Worzelish') 'What er you doin' roun' these 'ere parts?' kind of way.

Dusk was now falling, so I realised that finding a place to kip was becoming a pressing issue. Now, if you follow the road out of Easton-in-Gordano along St George's Hill, there is an old bit of road that eventually becomes a short cut for cyclists who wish to reach the roundabout over the M5. To the right of this is what I would describe as nothing more than a hedge, but in the great transformative tradition of TV's 'Stars in Their Eyes,' tonight it was going to be a bed.

I dived into a little clearing inside the bushes and commenced my attempt at roughing it. Remember, in these early days I used to take no groundsheet or pillow or anything like that - such things were for girls, or at least men with big rucksacks. *My* bed was just a sleeping bag flung flippantly onto the deck with the rucksack beneath my head as an uneven bit of cushioning.

As you can imagine, it took a long time to get to sleep. The close proximity to cars passing by on the A-road didn't help a lot, and at 1.25am I received a phone call from a friend in Mexico. Now that's a new one for you! Sadly, I couldn't answer the call as I didn't want to draw attention to myself to any nearby yokels tanked up on scrumpy cider.

At this point, the diary which I use as notes goes on to depict a collection of bizarre dreams, one of which involved waking up to find that everything was covered in snow. This reminded me of an experience I used to regularly have as a child, waking up (or at least thinking I'd woken up) to see everything doused in a surreal, white light, as though the entire world was made of cotton wool. It was a strange sensation that I imagine many hippies would go a great length to try to achieve by necking down all manner of illicit pills. The only 'pill' I'd encountered was the name of the nearby village.

As I go back further and further through my diary in order to write this book, the dream sequences become increasingly like memoirs from a double life that I can no longer remember. It seems that the brain can actually recall most real life experiences if prompted but dreams soon fade from memory. Indeed, if I browse through my diary entry for any day from the last decade, I can nearly always remember something that I've written about, yet most of the dreams I've noted down seem as foreign to me now as reading another person's diary altogether. To quote another Pink Floyd lyric, this time from the song Brain Damage, 'There's someone in my head and it's not me.'

They seem to have a lyric for everything somehow. No wonder people are willing to travel from Kent to Birmingham to sing their songs.

29) High in Glastonbury

Dawn broke, and after some patchy snoozing, I finally gave in to the traffic noise and decided to get up at 9.30am. It was another one of those 'Stephen Hawkins' moments again. Why did I choose that point to rise, rather than any other? Of course, it has to be because freedom of choice is just an illusion in the 4D particle universe. Remember?

I brushed my teeth and emerged from the bushes into another day, deciding to take a lane towards Nailsea from near the roundabout. I really wasn't expecting a 'killer hill' so early in the day. It seemed just to go on and on, like a highway to the stars. After this it was a downhill cruise on a B-road.

Nailsea is a small town, and I found my way to the centre, swiftly locating a café in a shopping centre. Making use of the toilet in the conveniently located supermarket next door (as is customary), I settled down for a slap-up breakfast and a cup of tea that went down like, well, you know what it went down like, don't you?

There was no time to delay though, as I had a lot of ticks to mark off my checklist today. The girl on the till seemed surprised when I said I was biking to Cheddar. 'It's not *that* far, surely?' I thought to myself.

I negotiated my way through the southern suburbs of the town and asked a passing milkman for directions to reach the lanes around Chelvey, from which point my map was detailed enough for me to continue.

I then followed a network of lanes that weren't too hilly, yet provided great views (surely the best combination – scenery without the strain), via Claverham, Yatton and Congresbury, where I decided to ingest some Lucozade for an energy boost. A group of youths were loitering on a bench outside the shop and I made a mental note that teenagers are much less threatening when they wear shirts, have hair on their heads and speak with a West Country accent.

The terrain got hillier as I continued south towards Sandford, but from here on my ride would be easy, for there was another disused railway line for me to relish. This particular route was part of Bristol and Exeter Railway's Cheddar Valley Line, now known as the Strawberry Line Trail. The line closed in 1963 when Doctor Beeching was swinging his famous axe around.

It appeared that my map was out of date, as the trail now commences its southward journey at Yatton. Perhaps I could have saved myself a few hills. I found my way to the access point, and I remember Sandford being overlooked by the imposing ridge of the Mendip Hills. It was quite a straggling settlement, strung out along the various roads.

As the Strawberry Line Trail headed southward, it seemed largely unchallenged by the terrain, but beyond Winscombe, a tunnel was required. I chatted to a couple who were strolling near the entrance. That West Country friendliness was in evidence again.

To be honest, I was surprised to encounter this tunnel, as it wasn't clearly marked on my map, so it was a positive boon to again be pedalling through a dark, damp conduit towards that small circle of light at the end. This time a strip of LED lights along the tarmac led me through. This tunnel was much shorter than the one I'd encountered at Bristol.

Crossing the A38, which is the UK's longest two-digit road and also the subject of The Wurzels' song 'Rock Around the A38,' the trackbed continued to Axbridge. This was a picturesque place that reminded me of Ireland, with pastel shaded frontages to the buildings. The trackbed ride recommenced on the other side of the town and before long I was passing the perfectly round Cheddar Reservoir.

By now it was boiling hot and I sat on a bench for around ten minutes cooling off. I was tempted to walk a circuit of this lake which had high reeds around the edges and the odd fisherman thrown in for good measure (not literally), but in the end I decided to continue to Cheddar.

Right, let's talk 'cheese.'

Cheddar cheese is the most popular cheese in the UK, making up 51% of the market. You could say it was the UK's major stakeholder when it comes to cheese. It has occasionally been declared the most popular cheese in the world. Not bad for a small town in Somerset.

Although West Country Farmhouse Cheddar has been granted 'protected designation of origin,' the more general term 'Cheddar' hasn't, which means it can be produced just about anywhere. Traditionally to be called Cheddar cheese, it had to be produced within thirty miles of Wells Cathedral.

So why Cheddar? As well as the fertile agricultural nature of the area, the answer could lie in the caves, which are the ideal humidity and temperature for maturing cheese. More about them later.

I soon realised that I was now in a thronging tourist hotspot with coaches depositing their content (people) all over the place. I dived for cover in the nearest bar. Inside two men were tying themselves up in knots discussing temperature conversion. In the end I had to intervene and point out that Fahrenheit and Celsius are both the same at -40 degrees and that you merely reverse the digits for 61 and 82. After this, I gracefully retired to a seat on my own to prevent myself from appearing too smarmy.

After this, it was time to check out the gorge. The B3135, heading east from the town centre, winds its way furiously through the deep rocks. I briefly spoke to a man at the entrance to Cheddar's famous caves and asked how much a tour would cost, expecting it to be a fiver or something. When I received the reply 'Sixteen pounds,' I returned to my bike.

I soon gave up biking and took to walking, for the bottom of the long, sustained climb up out of the gorge appears to be the 'business end' of the ascent. The views of the rock faces were stunning, and at one point I found a nice, cool cave that hadn't yet been subjected to commercialisation, and stood in it for a few minutes, enjoying the cool shade - the *free,* cool shade.

At its deepest point the gorge is around 450 feet deep. It is believed to have been carved out by meltwater floods from the ice ages over the last 1.2 million years. Interestingly, there is no river in the gorge today until you get near the bottom, because much of the water flowed underground creating the caves.

After my cool-off in the cave, I decided to attempt to cycle the rest of the climb if I could. The road takes around five miles to reach its summit, at which point the scenery becomes fairly flat and open – a plateau if you like. The speedo on my bike showed that I had tackled this incline at a steady pace of eight miles per hour, so it was just a plod really, but nevertheless I gave myself a metaphorical pat on the back.

I passed through Priddy (which sounds like an American mispronunciation) and soon reached the southern edge of the ridge, opting to rest a while at the viewpoint, observing the cars coming in and out of the gravel parking area. Then it was time to descend all the way down to Wookey Hole - a continuous freewheel of about thirty miles per hour, from open countryside into the land of the trees.

The caves at the bottom are perhaps almost as famous as those at Cheddar and carry a similarly astronomical entry fee. I inquired about doing the tour but ended up settling for a Turkish delight flavour ice cream which had a surprisingly accurate flavour.

Similar to Cheddar, these caves remain a constant temperature – 11 degrees Celsius or 52 degrees Fahrenheit. The Wookey Hole Witch is in fact not a crinkly old woman but a human-shaped stalagmite. Folklore says that it was a witch who was turned to stone by a monk called Father Bernard from nearby Glastonbury in the Dark Ages when the villagers sought help, blaming her for everything that went wrong.

In actual fact the skeleton of an old woman was discovered in the caves in 1912, so the legend may not be quite as daft as it sounds. Naturally, the story has been cashed in on and in 2009 an advert seeking an applicant to play the Wookey Hole Witch made national headlines.

Next on my tick-list was Wells, which unless you count the City of London as an individual entity, is England's smallest city, with a population of around 12,000. Close in the running are Ely, Ripon, Truro and surprisingly, Chichester. The *UK's* smallest city is St David's in Wales. With a population of less than 2,000 people you would be forgiven for calling it a village.

It was just a couple of miles to the city, and as I rode in I thought, 'That cathedral isn't much,' only to realise that it was just a parish church. When I reached the cathedral, I chained up my bike and set off to explore on foot.

The Vicar's Close nearby impressed me. Indeed, it is often quoted to be the oldest residential street remaining entirely intact in Europe. It dates from the middle of the 14th century and the tapered width of the road plays with perspective, making it look longer from one end than the other – a technique often used by Hollywood studios to create street scenes.

Wells itself was a settlement in Roman times, most probably due to the springs in the area. It is the thirteenth century cathedral that acquired city status for the place which remains to this day. However, Wells is lacking something that most cities have – a railway station. At one point it had three, but the final one closed in 1963, falling foul of Doctor Beeching's infamous flying axe.

And so, as I left the city, I found another piece of disused rail line to explore, this being a short section beside the A371 heading south-east, away from the settlement.

I then crossed this road and used the rural lanes to reach Glastonbury. The terrain is flat around here, with the imposing green mound of the famous tor overlooking the marshy agricultural land like a beacon. From the myriad drainage ditches, I could imagine this land once being covered by water. Adge Cutler and the Wurzels used to sing 'There ain't no ferry to Glastonbury,' but maybe they were just sailing upon a sea of cider!

The lane known as Long Drove headed in a dead straight line westward for a few miles, with the tor to my left, until I reached the A39 – that epic road that runs from Bath to Falmouth. I followed it as it bypassed much of the town with a sweeping curve. I then entered Glastonbury from the west. My stomach was leading the way as evening beckoned, and I now looked for a suitable place to eat.

Securing my bike to a trusty lamppost, I wandered down the sloping shop-lined street to a pub, where a 'curry night' was in full swing. Initially I just popped in for a drink, but was enticed by the affable price for a poppadom and my pick of five different dishes.

In that usual Somerset way, people started chatting, but these were incomers – the Kentish invasion! There seemed to be some kind of party taking place and a man with a south-eastern accent spoke first, followed by a sunburnt Czech girl who once lived in Maidstone (Kent's county town). The only local accent to be heard was that of the barman, and he looked a lot like a cousin of mine who lived in the same village as me. So I wonder, if you take the Man of Kent (or the Kentish Man) out of Kent does he cease to behave in a Kentish (i.e. pathologically shy) way?

As I left I had a nagging feeling that I'd ended up paying for an extra drink, but I didn't want to cause a fuss as the pub had been so friendly, so reunited with my bike, I headed off up the hill out of the centre of town in search of a suitable place to camp.

At the top of the hill I wandered around a field, but it seemed too open and visible for me to find a conducive spot. I returned to the lane and retreated back down the hill a bit, finding a bushy embankment beside the road. Hoping that the line of vision of passing drivers would be on the road and not looking to see if anybody was camping on the embankment, I surmised that I would be generally out of sight here, but as I settled among the large-leafed plants halfway up the slope, it became apparent that this was about as comfortable as a bed of nails. I had yet to learn that camping on a slope is a big no-no.

In spite of my attempts to rest, the sandman was not going to pay me a visit here, so I packed everything away again and returned to the lane, bathed in the glow of an orange streetlight as I pedalled back up the hill. The problem was that it was now dark and the need for somewhere to sleep was becoming quite pressing. I headed right out of the town this time, passing the tor on my right. There were plenty of fields here, but there were also plenty of hippies. Camper vans lined the road and I made a mental note not to try to camp in Glastonbury within a week of the music festival again.

I've always liked the hippy ethos of 'peace and freedom with guitars' whilst despairing of soulless 'dog eat dog' commercialism, so in a way these very adventures could be describes as kind of hippyish. However, I just wanted somewhere quiet to sleep, undisturbed by people having visions of pink rhinos coming out the ground on fountains of liquid gold, and yellow hippopotamuses floating down from the sky on clouds made of bright blue candy floss.

It seems as though I've actually just described the kind of scene you might find in Walt Disney's 'Fantasia' rather than what you might see if you've just ingested a load of lysergic acid diethylamide in the middle of a field in Somerset, but you get my point I'm sure.

As the lane descended the other side of the hill, I realised that if I went too far I'd be back in the land of flat, marshy open fields - definitely not ideal terrain for camping, unless you want to risk being run over by a tractor or scooped up by a combine harvester. Luckily, as I neared the bottom of the slope, I saw a disused orchard on my right.

I headed for the lowest corner of the orchard in order to be as far away from the road as possible, and located a fallen tree trunk to hide behind. However, on the other side of my sleeping bag was a rather large cowpat, and not even a large amount of illicit narcotics would make one of those hippies think rolling over into that could be pleasant, so I placed a log over it to act as a barrier, laid out my sleeping bag and prepared to snooze.

This was far more comfortable than the embankment had been, but as I lay looking up at the sky, the revellers were reaching their zenith up on the tor. I could hear loud voices shouting and shrieking into the night air. Who knows what phantasmagorical visions they were having up on that mound? It was surreal enough just hearing it.

However that washy feeling of sleepiness eventually overcame me, and I was placed into that bizarre world of dreams once again. My conclusion is thus. Why do people pay for substances, that have no doubt been sourced using methods contrary to their own ethics (something you will ironically have less qualms about if you are a pure, dyed in the wool, true blue, capitalist) in order to be submerged in a world of visions and confusion, when your brain provides this service for you completely free of charge every night? Maybe that's where the hippie generation went wrong.

30) Battling to Bridgwater

Spots of rain began to pitter-patter on my sleeping bag at about 4.30am. I tried to ignore them and snuggled in deeper, but there was no let-up and eventually I had to concede that this was it as far as sleep was concerned for that night. As it got light, a woodpigeon began making a strange noise consisting of a wheeze followed by a single deep coo. It sounded like it needed a shot of Ventolin.

The rain intensified, so I decided to walk to the top of the tor while I still had the chance to do so in relative comfort, in case a torrential downpour was brewing. The path wound its way around the green hillside, which had formed when the surrounding softer land was eroded, leaving only the hard sandstone in place.

The path seemed to wind and spiral its way to the summit. This was crowned with the remains of St Michael's Tower, which is just the empty tower of a 14th century church. The tor was known as Ynys yr Afalon, which means the Isle of Avalon. There is a myth that Joseph of Arimathea came to England and chose Glastonbury as his base from which to convert the English to Christianity and that he placed the Holy Grail beneath a spring on Tor Hill.

The other legend surrounding the town concerns King Arthur, who is recorded as falling at the Battle of Camlann in the sixth century AD. In 1191 monks at Glastonbury Abbey claimed to have found the aforementioned king's bones there, along with those of his queen, Guinevere.

As I stood at the top looking down across the orange dots of Glastonbury's streetlights, the sentiment was one of majestic triumph. The skies were moody and grey, but a line of brighter sky in the south was slowly moving closer. And what's more, I now had another tick to put on my balance sheet.

Heading back down, I decided that the sliver of bright sky was enough to propel me into another day's biking. The nearest railway station was about twenty miles away in Bridgwater, so it was a real case of biting the bullet or drowning trying.

I cruised down the hill to the A361 – yes, the same A361 that we encountered near Rugby and in the chapters on Avebury – and headed west, passing Glastonbury town once again before the road united with the A39 to bridge the River Brue to the neighbouring settlement of Street, which has a shoe museum.

"Take all the shoes and put 'em in a shoe museum!" - oh no, that was trees, wasn't it?

The reason for this fascination with footwear is that the Clark family commenced their sheepskin and shoe-making business in Street, before going 'hell for leather' and becoming the footwear chain we know today.

There was a conveniently placed McDonald's on the outskirts, and I waited for the doors to open at 7am so I could satiate myself with a 'Big Breakfast.' Once I had savoured the sausage patty, scrambled egg, muffin and hash brown (as opposed to 'brown hash' which was probably still being savoured by those hippies up on the tor), I grabbed my velocipede and continued through the centre of Street and out the other side, rejoining the busy A39 via the village of Walton, and departing towards Greinton when the A361 decided to part company from its two-digit accomplice.

I'd soon had enough of main roads and continued westward on a lane towards Moorlinch. I'd briefly donned my cycle helmet for the main road section and now took it off to let my head breathe again. At this time I had a strange notion that I would only damage my cranium if I fell off my bike on a major road.

I was surprised to find a school bus looming at me from around the bend on such as tiny lane, and I paused to take a photo as I crossed the dead straight waterway known as Kings Sedgemoor Drain. The scenery was very agricultural with the odd slope rising from the marshland. This was proper Wurzel country.

When I reached Chedzoy (how 'Somerset' does that name sound?), I paused to read that the famous Battle of Sedgemoor had taken place nearby in 1685, this being the climax of a protestant rebellion against Charles II by the Duke of Monmouth. This was the last time that the English fought the English on English soil.

I long for the day when an alien can visit the earth and read that a certain battle was the last time that humans fought humans on the human planet, but as I get older such innocent hopes fade. I've always hoped that human intelligence can eventually evolve sufficiently to do away with our competitive view of life, which is surely what the fighting is all about, but thinking about it, nature itself is competitive; species rise and fall according to survival of the fittest, and human behaviour is really just a natural extension of this.

I still like to think that we can transcend it one day, for we cannot possibly imagine the kind of civilisation that humans will have in a thousand years time. Or can we? Is it set in stone that it will still be based around money and power? Or can we use our intelligence to evolve beyond this?

You may recall much earlier that I mentioned the cost of having intelligent life in the universe. Sadly, having developed brains allows humans to inflict calculated pain on one another. The existence of torture must surely be the worst side effect of having intelligence? Animals mostly kill for food, but no animal behaves with such calculated cruelty. Increasingly I think the price of intelligence is too high in terms of suffering and that it would be better if intelligent life simply didn't exist. So far I've managed to do my part to back up this sentiment with action (or inaction) in not having any children, and in spite of heading rapidly towards married life I intend to keep it that way. No child of mine is going to commit genocide or pull the legs off of a crane fly for fun!

Having sneaked in that summation of our place in the universe, it is appropriate that my next stop was for a Galaxy 'Yuk' drink. The lane had reached the A39 near a motorway bridge and I soon found myself riding into the suburbs of Bridgwater.

I remember lots of terraced houses passing by in a blur as I rode towards the railway station. This clearly wasn't a tourist orientated place. As I waited in the booking hall for the train to Bristol, which would arrive at roughly 10am, I decided that I would have another look at Bath. My brain was taking control, sending me back in the same way that a teacher might return a child's homework saying, "Sorry, you haven't done it properly. Go back and try again."

Yet strangely upon reaching the spa city, my diary notes say little about what I actually did there, other than frequenting a Wetherspoons pub to eat a baguette containing some chicken in a stilton and mushroom sauce. 'Par for the course,' you are probably thinking.

I snoozed on the train to London in spite of the noise emanating from a gaggle of people who got on at Swindon. Upon alighting, I rode through Hyde Park and down The Mall to Charing Cross. At the time, the high speed service from Kent to London was still a pipe dream, so I was used to the slow crawl for an hour and a half from Charing Cross to Ashford via myriad towns and villages.

However, I will add that this particular entry to London from the coast is far more impressive than the one provided by the high speed line, as there are views across to the towers of Canary Wharf as well as the city, with its 'love it or hate it' gherkin.

All these towers were eclipsed by The Shard in 2013 which was briefly the tallest building in Europe, topping out at a little over a thousand feet. However Russia was having none of this and soon eclipsed it with the Mercury City Tower, the Eurasia Tower, the OKO South Tower and under construction at the time of writing, the Federation Vostok Tower, all in Moscow. This statement roughly translates as, "Take that and party!"

Well, I'm not sure if we want to get into a vertical equivalent of the arms race, especially as all this really achieves is getting some CEO with an already inflated ego even closer to the stratosphere. In fact it all seems rather reminiscent of the TV drama 'Northern Lights' which saw two neighbours trying to outdo each other with the Christmas lights outside their homes until they reached the point of despising each other.

I guess all this just galvanises the point made earlier about human competitiveness being sewn into all of us. For us mere mortals, we sometimes want our villages, towns and countries to be greater than others – to achieve by proxy the success that we cannot find for ourselves. Perhaps even the most peaceable of us are still drawn into this competitiveness to some degree, for when our ideas are threatened we can get pretty angry defending them. Maybe even those hippies on that hill at Glastonbury are not immune to this, once the bright green antelopes stop galloping out from under their eyelids.

Well, I didn't want this chapter to become a requiem for the perennial human hope of lasting peace; it just turned out that way. After this particular ride, I would have just one night sleeping in a bed, before meeting those three camping buddies for a night in 'our wood.' It felt quite strange to go from one style of camping to another, and took a little while to adapt to such decadence and luxury. My 'back to basics' style of camping is quite rapid in pace, pedalling from place to place, extracting all the available tourist kudos and then moving on, until the lack of light forces you to sleep. Meanwhile 'glamping' with those friends of mine involves moving no further than a few hundred yards all weekend, and that's just to collect firewood in order to ruminate around the blaze until dawn.

I felt that this particular trip had been a huge success, with so many West Country places I'd always wanted to see now checked off my list. So for now, you leave the four friends sitting around a rip-roaring fire, drinking wine from plastic glasses and tucking into the occasional snack, with the crackle of burning wood echoing round the trees, and the smoke rising steadily through the leafy branches, filling the night air and mingling with our laughter and semi-coherent conversations. Now that's living!

SOUTHERN HOME COUNTIES

31) Haslemere Hospitality

We now rewind a whole year and the month is June. Firstly I must congratulate you, my reader, for travelling so far with me. We have now reached the 'Ground Zero' from which all the journeys you have read about sprang, for this was my very first attempt to combine my dual interests of cycling and sleeping in hedges. This was the birth of a new hobby, and a phoenix which rose from the ashes of a previous hobby – playing in a pub rock band, which ironically was called Soaring Phoenix. It didn't so much soar as spontaneously combust. More later.

So at the time I embarked on this mission, apart from teenage scout camps, you could pretty much count the nights I'd spent sleeping outdoors on your phalanges.

I've told you a little bit about a hike from Kent to Somerset that I undertook in May 2006 with a guy called Tom. The idea for this was cooked up in the bar of a local pub when he said that he fancied spending the summer busking around the West Country like some kind of latter day travelling minstrel. I decided to walk as far as a village near Glastonbury with him, purely because it had the same name as our own, and then I'd leave him to it and come home on the train to a nice, warm bed.

Prior to this we thought we'd better have a practice run, with a local hike over a weekend. We ambled to the Kentish town of Tenterden (famed for being the possible birthplace of William Caxton, a pioneer of printing in England, and also once home to the Victorian actress, Dame Ellen Terry). We ended up camping in a wood near the village of Bethersden. Naturally this was after some hearty ale consumption in the boozer. As we lay in the warm, orange glow of a searing hot fire, I realised that there was something very enticing about drifting off like this, with the occasional crackle stirring us from the approaching slumber. The satisfaction was perhaps enhanced by suddenly seeing a whole new avenue of pleasure opening up – it was not only possible to sleep away from home without shelling out for a B&B or hotel; it also seemed pretty safe.

The pair of us camped for a total of thirteen nights during that hike, which varied from unseasonably hot spring sunshine to a watery purgatory. Perhaps disheartened by the fact that there is naff all to do in the microscopic Somerset village of Ham Street,

Tom promptly abandoned the busking idea and returned to Kent to try to live off the land for a while. He eventually met his wife and plugged back into mainstream living, but for me, I wanted more of this camping lark (for the days of regular camping in that hallowed 'glamping wood' were still a matter of years away at this point).

My first solo attempt was when I tentatively decided to return to that wood near the village of Bethersden, for a single night. The intention was for a bit of nostalgia revisiting The Bull pub. Now, if you've been doing your maths, that brings the total of nights I had camped to fifteen at the start of the trip I'm about to describe (unless you count scout camps from my teenage years, but let's keep it simple, right?).

The decision to have a proper solo adventure was made two days after my sister's June wedding. After many years of cycling out on day trips, getting progressively further away from home, I had found myself pushing the very limits of what can be done during a day using trains and a bike. It was time to break free of the gravitational pull of home and dive headlong into the depths of the vast unexplored wilderness of, er... Guildford!

However, my day began with a tour of the local newspaper office in my home town of Ashford. I had been a local correspondent for a number of years and hadn't yet taken up the opportunity to see where my ramblings are processed. I will digress no further, and I was soon breezing through the Vale of Kent on the train to Tonbridge, where I grabbed a bite to eat. Tonbridge is the busiest railway station in provincial Kent thanks to its myriad commuters (Sevenoaks, Tunbridge Wells, Ashford and Dartford complete the top five at the time of writing).

The next train was to the Surrey town of Redhill, and beyond this, the train journey prompted a few memories of that legendary walk with Tom as it trundled through Nutfield, Redhill, Reigate and Dorking – all places we'd encountered when pounding The Greensand Way footpath.

I emerged from the carriage at Guildford, feeling a little like Scott of the Antarctic, or even Edmund Hillary leaving the base camp on Everest. I began pedalling southward, out of the town and down to the village of Shalford. It is from here that one can continue a little further southward on the A281 and pick up the disused railway line that eventually interpolates the Downs Link and runs all the way to Shoreham-by-Sea on the Sussex Coast; a classic among cycle routes.

Having explored this route before, I instead turned right after bridging the river, proceeding up a steep hill past Selbourne

House, and it struck me that I would probably visit the Hampshire village of the same name (but minus the 'U') sometime during this trip.

It is always nice to cycle on conduits that cars can't use, so when I reached the crossroads with the B2130, I continued ahead where vehicles were prohibited, and then turned left onto a lane called Hambledon Road. My route squeezed through the Surrey Hills in a deep cutting and unsurprisingly, I soon came to the village of Hambledon, another place I'd passed through during that hike to Somerset.

Beyond this, I negotiated my way to Witley Station and climbed northward up the hill before bridging the line and turning 180 degrees to continue via the village of Wormley, along a familiar lane to Brook. It was here that I made my first pub stop in an inn laying back from the A286 road. I must have been in a puritanical frame of mind as my diary is telling me that I had a ginger beer.

What – no real ale? This must be someone else's diary surely? I have visions of half my potential readers just slamming the book shut in disgust, thinking, 'He was talking about people selling their souls to Lucifer in the preface and now he's sitting there quaffing a ginger beer. I want my money back!' Well, just you hang on a minute; some serious 'manning up' was to follow.

After consuming the refreshing beverage on a bench at the front of the pub, the lane beyond was something of a rude awakening. I puffed my way up a steep incline, bearing right at the junction of Bowlhead Green, heading north towards the formidable A3.

These perspiration inducing climbs often give one a sense of honing body and mind. Such exertion must surely be burning calories as well as releasing those 'feel good' endorphins. The simple equation for staying thin is 'calories burned = calories consumed.'

I am reminded of my wafer-thin camping buddy who will spend much of his weekend in the woods reading the nutritional info on food packaging while paradoxically turning a blind eye to any such details on the cans of beer and bottles of wine. Yet, following the British food scandal, one can't help but wonder how manufacturers can know the exact quantities of fat, protein, carbohydrate, etc. to the nearest fraction of a gram when they don't even know if they are giving us cow or horse.

Leaving the lane, I took a bridleway past a stately looking house which appeared to have its own lake, a far more pleasant status symbol than a BMW or an unfeasibly large TV screen in my opinion, especially if you get a few swans bunged in at no extra cost.

Somehow I managed to cross the dual carriageway A3, but whether or not I made a death defying, two-stage, kamikaze sprint across or used a more sensible method like using a bridge (if there was one), I have no idea. I've got a feeling it was the former option somehow. I then briefly used part of the Old Portsmouth Road, which would have been the A3 in quieter days, and then branched off onto a little lane to head into the tiny village of Thursley. Peace again.

I followed The Street southward as it passed the church and eventually reached a dead end, where the Greensand Way took over as a gravelly track. I now faced an epic climb to Hindhead, for in front of me was the curving wooded ridge of the Devil's Punchbowl, which provides fantastic views all around. It must now be much more peaceful due to the diversion of the A3 via a tunnel.

The trail climbed via shady cuttings through the trees, emerging into open heathland for the final ascent to the summit. In these days, it crossed the A3 (now in single carriageway mode) and then followed the southern edge of the ridge round as it curved westward towards Hindhead Village.

I headed straight for the National Trust café and sat outside with a pot of tea, taking it the fresh, high altitude air, with the incessant rush of traffic in the background. Maps on the wall illustrated the route of the proposed Hindhead Tunnel and anticipated the future restoration of tranquillity to this beauty spot.

Still on the 'hiking nostalgia' trail, I then shed all this accumulated height in cruising down the A287 road towards Shottermill, turning off onto lanes and backstreets to negotiate my way to a familiar spot where I had camped with Tom. This was at a location just off the Greensand Way which was just a narrow footpath at this point. The thistle bushes were still there and just as thorny.

Beyond this, I asked for directions to Haslemere town centre from a number of people, stating that I intended to follow the Greensand Way to reach it. The blank stares and statements that they had never heard of the long distance path took me by surprise. How can you live in Haslemere and not know the Greensand Way? After all, this 110-mile path from Hamstreet in Kent reaches its conclusion in the town. My fiancée informs me that she once knew somebody who had lived in London for many years without once seeing The Tower of Big Ben, so I guess I shouldn't be so shocked.

I eventually arrived in the central shopping street and chained up my bike, ready to explore the town. This is of course a euphemism for popping into The White Horse for a beverage or two.

The barman was a young, affable chap who had the air of a university graduate filling in with a bit of bar-work. To show how wrong I might have been, I have a friend who is a lifelong farmer who exudes a similar ambience. I would say that anybody who throws 'Yeah yeah yeah' into a conversation at regular intervals qualifies for the 'university type' epithet, as does any use of the Australian-style raised pitch at the end of sentences. Stereotypically most farmers opt for the more Wurzelish (or Worzelish) 'ooh aah,' but then we don't want to propagate stereotypes here, so we?

I asked what time food was served and it appeared that I would have to wait until early evening for the kitchen to open. However, I'd already mentioned that the pub is featured in one of my books (which documents the aforementioned hike that I keep carping on about), and upon seeing me scribbling down some notes at a table, he informed me that dinner time had been moved back half an hour, thus securing a good report should any book be written about this bike ride. What an adept young man he was, for I had no intention of any kind of write-up at this point.

For the lone traveller chatty bar staff are a godsend, representing an oasis of conversation and a feeling of acceptance. I was pleased to sit at the bar and talk about where I was from and what I was doing in Haslemere. It turned out that the young man had lived in a Kentish village not too far from my home. Those Kentish folk are getting everywhere these days. Anyway, in spite of the accommodating service, I decided against the notion of dining here and opted to get a take-away further along my route. Everybody has got to have a diva-ish moment occasionally.

The trip down memory lane continued, as I followed the exact route that I'd hiked westward out of the town via Shottermill, passing into Hampshire near Hammer and crossing the road bridge to the north side of the A3. I realise that for my reader, this is becoming a little like the film 'Back to the Future II' – a sequel so full of references to its predecessor that it is barely incomprehensible as a stand-alone work. I promise that we will reach some new territory soon.

Dusk fell as I pedalled via the village of Bramshott. During this section of the ride, I remember passing a number of pubs and wondering what kind of revelry was taking place inside, perhaps forgetting that it was Monday night. I briefly headed north on a B-road, before taking the wide lane towards Whitehill. This eventually settled on a dead straight course through the trees. 'Faux Roman' if you like.

At the crossroads with the similarly straight main road down from Bordon, I headed up to the Chinese takeaway and purchased a spring roll and a can of Coke. I was positively relishing this re-enactment by bike, for the miles were just falling away, and what had taken a day on foot, could be knocked off in just a matter of hours.

As I well knew, the course of the dead straight lane, continued westward beyond the junction, initially lined with houses, before narrowing into a dead end and becoming a byway across a golf course. I then followed the lane towards Selborne. I would soon reach a wooded bank on my left-hand-side. This handy piece of knowledge eliminated the need to search for somewhere suitable to camp, which as we already know can vary from 'serendipitous' to 'fraught.' However, a bankside location such as this is never ideal due to the incline.

So sans tent, sans groundsheet, sans anything, I headed into the leafy woodland and laid my sleeping bag out for the night. Soon I was laying there, enjoying the peace and anticipating the hooting of owls. Instead, I spotted a badger traipsing through the leaves. Sometimes roughing it like this is a great way to see nature up close; other times its just a great way to get soaked.

Today I had learned that a former MP of Haslemere founded the US colony of Georgia. I had also ridden 32 miles. This was surely enough exercise for body and mind for any day.

32) Meon's Monsters

I awoke early, disturbed by the sound of yapping dogs. There must have been a kennel near here. Either that or just a household with a penchant for canines. I stuffed my sleeping bag back into my rucksack and returned down the bank to the lane, to continue my merry way to Selborne.

I recall a gentle descent to the village past some buildings with a stately feel. The public toilets came in very handy and I briefly joined the B-road heading northward. Selborne's most famous resident was the famous naturalist Rev. Gilbert White, whose home has been converted into a museum which also contains an exhibition on the life of Captain Lawrence Oates and his uncle Frank Oates, who was also an explorer.

Robert Falcon Scott's exhibition to the South Pole is famous for the all the wrong reasons. Firstly, the five-man team reached the pole on January 18th 1912, only to find that a party led by the Norwegian explorer Roald Amundsen had got there just over a month earlier and left their camp behind as proof – perhaps the ultimate statement of 'Take that and party!'

All joking aside now, for it was on the return trip that things took a tragic turn. Firstly one of the team died, possibly from brain damage incurred by a fall, and then Captain Oates began to suffer from severe frostbite. Viewing himself as a hindrance to the survival of the others who depended on reaching the food and fuel depot that had been laid in advance, he sacrificed his life. The captain is usually cited as uttering the lines, "I'm just going outside and may be some time," before walking out of the tent into a blizzard to a certain death.

However, the other three explorers died of starvation and exposure a short time later, trapped in their tent by a blizzard and unable to continue. They were just eleven miles short of their target.

After that little interlude, the rest of *my* story is going to seem a bit tame in comparison. I turned left onto a lane via Upper and Lower Farringdon and I recall some pleasant thatched cottages in the area. The last bit up to the village of Four Marks was a gruelling climb and I ended up surrendering to the incline and walked the last little bit up to the A31.

The village of Four Marks has a modern feel, being strung out along one of the single carriageway sections of this arterial road. There are ample shops and amenities, and I popped into a bakery for a toasted sandwich and a life affirming 'Yuk' drink. I got chatting to the lady behind the counter about my challenge and she said that she had a tent in her garden that I could have camped in. It seemed that I was in a friendly area.

There was no rest for the wicked though, and I headed south-west on the main road before turning right onto a byway which took me across to a lane via the little village of Bighton. After more pedalling I turned right onto a B-road just to the north of New Alresford. I was presented with another epic climb and some woodlands. I'm not sure to what extent I was just getting tired, but for an area with no really remarkable views the ascents seemed awfully challenging. The countryside was generally that of large, open, rolling fields.

I branched off onto a byway which undulated over some open, stately looking land, passing Northington Grange, an impressive building with columns which is used as an opera house. A left turn at the end of the trail took me south towards Itchen Abbas, and I was pleased to be able to pick up a short section of disused railway line running westward behind the village. I had to push my bike up the bank to reach a bridge and then continued my journey towards Winchester on the B-road.

After bridging the M3 between Martyr Worthy and Abbots Worthy, I came to Kings Worthy. There is also a Headbourne Worthy nearby, so it appears that an awful lot of worthy people once dwelled in this area.

It was here that I spotted a pub on the opposite side of the A33, namely Darcy's Coach and Horses. I would have immediately lowered the tone of what seemed quite a posh establishment by walking in with my rucksack. I opted for some olive bread and nuts as a simple but classy snack, and on a table next to me there were a couple of old ladies complaining that the pepper wasn't ground finely enough.

Such pedantry reminded me of Basil Fawlty's quote in the classic comedy Fawlty Towers; "Would you like a tea cosy for your pepper-pot, perhaps?" I would have loved to hear one of my camping pals reply to them with that stock phrase of theirs, 'You wanna man up a bit!'

It was at this point that I changed my route and doubled back. I think I'd had enough of memory lane and seen a lifetime's quota of long, expansive hillsides. I was missing the more close-knit countryside of the east, with its small fields and scattered woodlands.

So I headed back the way I came and took a lane southward, bridging the River Itchen to another little village – Easton. Beyond this, it made another ascent worthy of Edmund Hillary. The sustained heat finally got to me and I capitulated to rest, diving into the bushes and entering another world. This little grotto seemed to be the perfect campsite.

Waking up and doing a load of updates to my village website at 4am the previous day no doubt helped to weary me, and I flirted with the idea of just staying here for the rest of the day. I laid down, using my rucksack as a pillow and before long the sandman had arrived and escorted me to the land of Nod. Unfortunately this spot wasn't quite as blissful as it seemed, as every time a car passed by on the tarmac just a few feet away, I was roused back to the land of Unnod. That said, this afternoon snooze was much needed and provided me with the welcome surge of energy I needed to continue.

I eventually dragged myself out of the bushes and up the remainder of the hill. At the top I discovered a conveniently placed pub, which would have been ideal for an evening meal had I completely conked out in the hedgerow.

From the roundabout, I descended back towards Winchester on the A31, before branching off on the A272, which steadily climbed onto the ridge to join the South Downs Way heading east. But this time the effort seemed worth it, for the views were nothing short of stunning.

I soon came to a place called Cheriton which prompted me to stop and text a few people from the Folkestone area in Kent, for there is a district of the same name there. More interesting was that this was the site of a battle in the time of Charles I; March 29th 1644 to be precise. The battle was during the English Civil War and the Royalists had driven the Parliamentarians eastward from the West Country. However, the Parliamentarians defeated the Royalists in the Battle of Cheriton.

I guess it's a little like the way a swathe of blue or red can sweep across areas of the country on election night and then the following election, it is driven back again. The only difference is, these days it is done with votes instead of human lives. At least some things have improved.

I continued along the main road. The miles were flying by now and I soon reached a pivotal crossroads with the A32. The pub, Meon Hut, is sometimes marked on maps here. It is now a chain pub and I stopped for a ginger beer. I was making a habit of this.

After this light refreshment I continued along the A272 to a point where the road runs through a brick tunnel. You will recall that subterranean riding is like the 'royal flush' of cycling; an opportunity that comes up once in a blue moon. I cycled through and back again, relishing the novelty. This east-west tunnel runs beneath the trackbed of the former north-south Meon Valley railway line. As if on a giant elastic band, I then returned to the pub and settled down for a steak and ale pie, before heading back towards that tunnel again.

I managed to find a way up onto the embankment to explore the old rail route. It's all a bit hazy, but I seem to recall a track with piles of logs beside it at the bottom of the cutting. I considered camping on the actual trackbed, but as I surveyed the area, the ground suddenly shook with what seemed like heavy footsteps. What could this be – an earthquake? A rhino escaped from a local zoo? Immediately this new panacea / outdoor hobby seemed less of a good idea. Was I in danger?

Just as I looked up, I just caught a glimpse of the backside of a huge wild boar disappearing into the woodland below. To use another one of those camping sayings, I thought, 'Blow this for a game of darts' and immediately continued southward along the embankment. Being sat on by a half-ton derriere in the middle of the night was definitely not on my 'to do' list.

After a while the terrain levelled out, and as the grassy trackbed curved westwards, it began to go into a cutting. I wheeled my bike along this section which clearly wasn't intended for public use, and I had to skirt up the bank a few times to avoid the stagnant puddles and the bushes.

After about three quarters of a mile I decided to climb to the top of the bank to see if there was anywhere suitable to camp up there. After all, laying in putrid water while rats scurry around wasn't my idea of fun, and contracting Weil's disease was not on my 'tick list' any more than a close encounter with that wild boar was.

Thankfully, there was a nice, smooth surface at the top. It was a considerable challenge hauling my bike up there, but somehow I managed it and soon I was nestled beneath the trees, the trunks of which were neatly preventing me from rolling down the bank.

A songbird was making a melodious whistle as dusk fell and I tried to drift away. However, my night was disturbed by an eerie shrieking. This was the same creature that Tom and myself had christened the 'terror hog' on our long walk. Uncertain if it was a wild boar or just a badger, we'd spent a couple of edgy nights laying there, wide awake with pounding hearts, waiting for the disturbing sound to recede.

This time was just the same; the deranged calls started off as a sound invading my subconscious, reaching a climax with me waking up. The howls gradually decreased in volume as the creature took its night-time prowl elsewhere. It was as though the devil himself was stalking the woods at night, striking fear into the hearts of unsuspecting campers.

With peace restored I eventually got back off to sleep, and the peculiar thing is that while I have heard the call of foxes many times while camping (and they sound eerie enough), I have never heard this 'terror hog' noise again.

33) Derailing in Hayling

The lead singer of the pub band that I used to be in texted during the night. I'd lost touch with her for six months and learned that she'd recently been in hospital but seemed to be over the worst. I sent a few replies, and this seems an appropriate time to tell you about the craziest rock band ever to hit Kent.

It all began when the landlord of a local pub said that there was a drummer and a bass player jamming about in his shed. One of them would later be known as 'the godfather of glamping' and the other would eventually reveal his depression inducing devotion to Arsenal Football Club. I wandered out to join this 'chalk and cheese' type duo and add a bit of guitar. Thus the legendary Soaring Phoenix was born.

After several months of Tuesday night shed-jams, the landlord coerced us into doing a short performance in the bar area. However, the singer we had at the time had an attack of nerves, as did the drummer. He wasn't quite so godfatherly on this occasion.

Instead, my brother-in-law decided to pound the skins a bit and we blasted out some riffs. These were just that – riffs, not songs – and my uncle eventually bribed me with a free pint of beer if we could play something proper, as opposed to just the opening ten chord-stabs of 'Eye of the Tiger' played repeatedly for about four minutes.

The drummer got over his shyness but the singer didn't, so we acquired a new vocalist, this being the girl who had just texted me. We also added a rhythm guitarist (the 'phone a friend' friend in this book). Strangely enough, we were soon gigging twice a week, although we were never sure if the 'groupies' who followed us were genuine fans or just coming along to laugh at the histrionics, for there were numerous catatonic episodes such as the bass player's spare shirt ending up in a pool of drink and the laughable rage that resulted.

OK, it hardly compares with the drama associated with bands such as The Kinks, where a wrong note could reputedly earn you a smack round the chops, but it was pretty extreme for a pub band at times. Often I would throw in the towel on this dysfunctional combo, only to return for a few 'final' gigs (very 'Rolling Stones'). Meanwhile the rhythm guitarist would be having a diva-ish moment saying things like, "We can't play here because the pub has got dirty power," because the amplifiers were buzzing. I had no idea that electricity could be pure or sullied, but now I knew.

As tensions manifested, you could say that the Soaring Phoenix metamorphosed into the Warring Phoenix, and by the spring preceding this inaugural biking adventure it would become the Boring Phoenix, for it would no longer exist.

Following the dissolution of this band, I wondered what would replace it, for it had become a holistic lifestyle, with the five of us doubling as a social group cum 'pub quiz team' as well. The end of the band was like pulling the rug away to see what was still standing.

So you see, these cycling trips began as something of a diversion, but as you will have observed, the diversion would eventually become the *raison d'etre,* for these trips themselves became the phoenix that rose from the ashes of The Phoenix. To cut a long story short, I sent a few replies to my former bandmate over the course of the morning, which began healthily by wolfing down some apple slices and a few olives, before wandering back along the trackbed to the A272, and pedalling west to the crossroads with the A32.

This cross reminded me of one of those American places which consist of little more than a few services huddled around a road junction, as though clinging on for dear life. In the USA this would have a name like 'Meon Hut City.'

Heading south, I encountered a long, steep hill before turning left into the village of West Meon. A little path cut through to the beginning of the Meon Valley Trail, which heads southward on another section of the former trackbed. I sat on a bench and tucked into a Scotch egg just before receiving a phone call from a former rhythm guitarist with a dislike of impure electrical currents. I could never be the Ignoring Phoenix, so of course, I answered.

The Meon Valley Railway used to run for 22 miles from Alton (at the north end) to Fareham (to the south). Passenger services ceased in 1955. The cycle route is around ten miles long and the only evidence of a station that I spotted was where the path deviates around a building at Droxford, roughly halfway along this section.

In my notes I stated that there was 'an interesting bit where a lane just ended before the bridge under the railway but there was no evidence of a bridge over the river the other side.' I told you these recollections would get more hazy as the book goes on. From my map it appears that I was referring to West Street just south of Soberton.

Memory is funny, for I am now getting that feeling of disconnection that I had when reading details of my old dreams about my actual experiences. Is somebody ghostwriting my diary? Taking this musing further, if we don't remember something, does it cease to be an experience? After all, an experience is something that shapes who we are now because we remember it.

To take this one stage further, if one is frightened of visiting the dentist, one can take a sedative and simply not remember it, but does that mean that the experience was any less unpleasant than without the chemical cosh? Thinking of my horror writer friend again, I can imagine a plot where it is discovered that when we have a general anaesthetic for an operation, we experience everything that happens, but because we can remember none of it, it just feels as though we were blissfully unaware. Scary stuff, hey?

Now, the main part of the trail ended when it reached the A334 in the large village of Wickham. I decided it was time for a hearty breakfast and I quickly located a tea room in which to indulge myself. I recall the sausages being particularly tasty here.

After this, I explored the remaining mile or so of trackbed to the south of the road. This became progressively narrower as it neared the point where it would have joined the mainline from Eastleigh to Fareham. Reluctantly I turned myself around and opted for the A32 as my route to Fareham instead.

Heading south, I pounded up the long hill where the road has a 'crawler lane,' and as I descended to cross the M27, I entered a suburbia which would remain with me all the way to Havant, for I turned left in Fareham to follow the A27 eastward via Portchester. At the end of the M27, this road takes over the baton of 'South Coast Trunk Road' and freaks out into a dual carriageway, so I continued on B-roads which would have been part of the A27 prior to this upgrade.

Sometimes semi-urban roads like this can be a great way to knock off a few miles quickly, for the pace of the traffic just seems to keep you drifting along in the flow. However, what interested me at Havant was another old trackbed. I asked a passerby how to get to it and he replied, "Ah, Hayling Billy!" before pointing me in the right direction.

Hayling Billy was named after the engines that used it, and the route, which runs for just a few miles south to Hayling Island operated passenger services from 1867 to 1963. The main reason for the line's closure was because maintaining the bridge over the short channel onto the island was too expensive. You can still see the stumps where the crossing used to be.

Walkers and cyclists therefore have to use the main road bridge instead before rejoining 'Billy.' The trail took me across flat, marshy farmland, and I was soon coming into South Hayling, which is the commercial centre of this tiny island. I followed a straight, suburban road to the seafront from the point where the line's terminus would have been. The promenade was resplendent with all the usual attractions such as rides, candy floss and amusement machines in which to dispose of your spare cash, seduced by the sight of rotating images of fruit.

I didn't stay for long, but merely followed the A-road back out of the town towards the mainland via the village of Stoke, where I found a suitable pub in which to imbibe a pint of mild. Since this visit a pint of this dark, easy-going ale is becoming more of a luxury. It seems that the modern drinker isn't so interested in a tasty low alcohol beer as opposed to just getting absolutely plastered on high octane lager.

The interior of this pub was mellow and relaxing, and a relatively new album was drifting from the jukebox. The singer was a young lady from London known as Amy Winehouse. When I first heard Amy's hit song 'Rehab' on the radio I actually thought, 'This is a song from the sixties I've never heard before,' although I wasn't aware that such a thing as 'rehab' even existed in that fabled decade.

Up to this point in time, you could pretty much tell the decade a record was produced in by the overall sound, the drums in particular being the give-away, from the 'cardboard box' thud sound of the fifties to the massive reverberating snare sound of the eighties. It seemed that in the noughties technology and recording techniques reached a point where one could convincingly emulate the feel of any era at the touch of a button. As for Amy, this talented, albeit colourful and frank songwriter tragically joined the '27 club' a few years later, this being the age at which many a rock and pop legend has croaked.

With so many luminary names joining the 'great gig in the sky' prematurely, it seems that even as early as the sixties, morbid legends were springing up, even about rock stars who had yet to kick the bucket. The 'Paul McCartney is dead' conspiracy surrounding The Beatles was particularly odd. The registration of the VW Beetle on the Abbey Road album cover ends with '28IF.' Among other things, this was taken as evidence that Paul would be 28 *if* he was still alive. So here once and for all, Paul did not join the 27 club. In fact he's even too old for the 72 club now. The man is indestructible!

Now, as I sat at the bar I noticed something about the shape of Hayling Island – it looks like a mirror image of Great Britain. OK, the bit that would be Kent (in the west, as it's a mirror image) has been somewhat elongated, but if you look at a map you'll see exactly what I mean.

After this I decided to take a ride around the lanes in the north-east of the island via the villages of Tye, North Hayling and Northney. In our mirror image map, these would represent the west coast of Scotland. I was soon back off the island, having thoroughly 'done it.'

Back in 2013, Russian president Vladimir Putin's official spokesman Dmitry Peskov was alleged to have made a comment that "Britain is just a small island. No one pays any attention to them." Although he denied making the comment, I wonder if a visit to Hayling Island might have helped change such a perspective. Britain is the eighth largest island in the world, whilst Hayling Island fits the criteria of 'small island' very aptly, although I will add that it is actually the third largest English island after Wight and Sheppey.

Picking up the A259, which is a remarkably long road running all the way along the coast from Havant in Hampshire to Folkestone in Kent, I headed eastward. This road reminded me of the former prime minister Gordon Brown, waiting interminably for his chance to be prime minister while Tony Blair ruled for almost three terms. For the parallel A27 is getting all the glory in holding the title of South Coast Trunk Road, all the way from Havant until just north-east of Eastbourne, where the A259 finally seizes the baton, only to have it snatched away again just after it reaches Kent by the David Cameron of roads, that young upstart, the A2070.

I imagine that the personification of roads is a classifiable disorder, but I see no shame in it. There are plenty more harmful ideas that people cling onto to make sense of the vast ocean of data known as 'life.' And I don't think anybody has ever killed because they thought the A259 has a personality.

I continued into West Sussex via a string of villages located along the inlets that nose inland from the English Channel. Many a schoolboy will know the rude limerick about one of these villages that begins, 'There was an young man from Bosham...' Or was it Cosham?

I was soon in Chichester and headed straight for a trusty pub (no surprise there), enjoying a mixed bean chilli followed by a 'mint bomb' ice cream, all washed down with a glass of Leffe. Meanwhile some drunks argued about being refused more alcohol, perhaps reinforcing the point that they'd had enough.

As I wandered out, a spot of rain hit me and I observed that the sky was now grey. I made an executive decision to curtail the adventure and return home, but by now the seed had been sewn for all the expeditions in this book. I had another local night camping in those woods near Bethersden in Kent a month or so later and the following spring would be my first camp with three friends in the wood that we have since come to know as 'Mecca.' Time to indulge my imagination again.

Imagine if you will, waking up to the sound of birdsong and then looking up to realise that you are in a tent, that you don't have to go to work and that it is warm. You can see through the canvas that it is going to be a glorious sunny day.

You hear the sound of gentle crackling from the recently lit fire, coupled with the murmur of conversation and laughter from three of your best friends. This is pierced by the whistle of an old kettle boiling on the grate and the splutter of sausages sizzling in a pan. You unzip the tent to see the sun streaming through the trees in a shaft of hazy light and stumble to your feet, out into a glade surrounded by cherry trees, resplendent in young, fresh, green leaves.

You take your cup of tea and sit down in the chair, ready to feast on a hearty breakfast roll, knowing that in a few hours time you'll be hearing that first crack and hiss as you remove the ring-pull from a can of your favourite beer, pouring it into a rounded glass that nurtures a nice, creamy head. Then you take your first sip.

With all life's stresses and troubles, worries and fears, such moments are when you feel as though you are living the dream. Both the travels in this book and the camps with friends have provided a reliable source of pleasure during the ups and downs of the years. That first bike ride around the home counties took place at a time of uncertainty, whilst the most recent trip along the Basingstoke Canal was in a totally different epoch for me, with marriage on the horizon.

The moral of these tales, if any, is to find something you like and keep doing it, whatever else happens, like finding a crack of light in the darkness of mundanity and widening it, until you can look both backward and forward simultaneously, knowing that current adventures are the first of many and that you really have come 'the full cycle.'

EPILOGUE

Reader, I married her.

APPENDIX – Further Routes

Here I am going to list all other significant cycle routes that I have undertaken closer to home as day trips, which are therefore not documented in this book.

Rail to bike conversions

The Crab and Winkle Way from Canterbury to Whitstable (Kent) uses part of the trackbed of the world's first railway for paying passengers (opened 1830), although it is barely recognisable as a rail trail due to deviations in the route.

The Forest Way – Groombridge (Kent) to East Grinstead (East Sussex)

The Worth Way – East Grinstead to just east of Crawley (West Sussex)

The Cuckoo Trail – Polegate (East Sussex) to Heathfield. Don't forget to check out the Millennium Green in Heathfield, which extends the trail a mile north from the town, now accessed via a supermarket car park since the tunnel was closed following an alleged rape in 2005.

Downs Link – Head north from Shoreham-by-Sea (West Sussex) on the path by the River Adur to pick up the trail which runs to Shalford (Surrey) via Christ's Hospital and Cranleigh. The route is well signed up over the hillside at its only tunnel.

The Flitch Way runs from Braintree (Essex) westward almost as far as Bishop's Stortford (Herts) via Great Dunmow, where there is a diversion from the trackbed onto roads. The route runs close to Stansted Airport at the western end and one has to use roads for the last few miles into Bishop's Stortford.

Finsbury Park to Alexandra Palace (London) - consists of two short sections of trackbed which can be linked by skirting the edge of Highgate woods. Undertaken by myself on foot.

Canal routes

Royal Military Canal – you can link up the cycleway section which runs from Seabrook (Kent) to West Hythe with a two-mile 'unofficial' track section between the villages of Ruckinge and Hamstreet, using quiet country lanes. Cyclists should show particular respect on this latter section and walk if asked. This canal is the UK's third longest defensive structure, built as a line of defence against a feared Napoleonic invasion.

Regent's Canal – a link across London between the Grand Union Canal at Paddington with the River Lee Navigation at Limehouse. Passes by London Zoo and through Camden Market. The cyclist must negotiate the streets above ground at points where there are tunnels. Some sections are designated 'walking only' so pushing the bike is advised.

Other routes

Although the Pilgrims' Way footpath traditionally links Winchester and Canterbury, the prehistoric trackway would have run from the English Channel all the way to Avebury in Wiltshire. The section along the spring line of the North Downs can be traced as a combination of trackway and lanes from Postling in Kent to Titsey (near Oxted in Surrey). There is a detour from the ancient route for cyclists north of Ashford between Wye and Westwell. You can also link the sections on either side of the River Medway with the cycle route over the M2 bridge. The section west of Otford where it crosses the M25 takes considerable negotiation due to a complete lack of signage.

The Viking Coastal Trail forms a complete circle around the Isle of Thanet in Kent – actually a peninsula that fancies itself being surrounded by water. The route takes in Ramsgate, Broadstairs, Margate and the historic Roman ruins at Reculver.

The Heron Trail is a signed circuit of the Hoo Peninsula in Kent. The route will be considerably less enjoyable if Boris Johnson gets his dream of a massive airport here.

Garden Coast Sea Wall – Ride from Littlestone (Kent) to Folkestone along the long, curving bay. One has to use roads including the A259 between Dymchurch Redoubt and Hythe Seafront.

River Stour – National Cycle Route 18 follows the river through Ashford (Kent), and has an off-road section from Godmersham to Chartham where it rejoins the riverbank to Canterbury.

Bewl Water – A complete eleven-mile circuit of the largest lake in South-East England.

ACKNOWLEDGEMENTS

Books, websites and humans consulted or quoted in this book:

AA book of British Towns – Philip Llewelin/Ann Saunders (Drive Publications Limited)
Guinness Book of Answers – Norris McWhirter (Guinness Superlatives)
The Top Ten of Everything – Russell Ash (Queen Anne Press)
A Brief History of Time – Stephen Hawking (Bantam Books)
Dreamland – David K. Randall (W.W. Norton)
Revolution in the Head – Ian MacDonald (Pimlico)
Canal and River Trust Website
BBC Website
English Heritage Website
National Trust Website
National Trails Website
SABRE Road Website
Numerous websites on various towns, villages and routes visited or relating to specific subjects briefly touched upon, such as the Bath and Bristol Railway Path, the Thames Bridges and Richard III
Roger Colton (my father)

Other books by Adam Colton available in paperback and on Amazon Kindle:

England and Wales in a Flash (father and son jaunt around the mainland coast in search of every lighthouse)
Mud Sweat and Beers (two friends hike across Southern England from Kent to Somerset documenting their adventure)
Bordering on Lunacy (father and son explore the lighthouses of Southern Scotland and trace the route of the border with England)
Conundrum (collection of short stories set at iconic Kentish locations with dark twists and dystopian undertones)*

* Paperback release as 'Seven Dreams of Reality' and 'The Kent-erbury Tales'